Denver Broncos: Top 5 of Everything

Ranking the Top Players, Greatest Games and Wildest Moments in Broncos History

Chris Bradshaw

St Cyprian Books

Copyright © 2023 by Chris Bradshaw

All rights reserved.

No portion of this book may be reproduced in any form without written permission from the publisher or author, except as permitted by U.S. copyright law.

This publication is designed to provide accurate and authoritative information in regard to the subject matter covered. It is sold with the understanding that neither the author nor the publisher is engaged in rendering legal, investment, accounting or other professional services. While the publisher and author have used their best efforts in preparing this book, they make no representations or warranties with respect to the accuracy or completeness of the contents of this book and specifically disclaim any implied warranties of merchantability or fitness for a particular purpose. No warranty may be created or extended by sales representatives or written sales materials. The advice and strategies contained herein may not be suitable for your situation. You should consult with a professional when appropriate. Neither the publisher nor the author shall be liable for any loss of profit or any other commercial damages, including but not limited to special, incidental, consequential, personal, or other damages.

First edition 2023

Contents

Introduction and Selection Criteria ... 1

Players ... 4

1. Top 5 Quarterbacks ... 5
2. Top 5 Running Backs ... 10
3. Top 5 Wide Receivers ... 14
4. Top 5 Pass Rushers ... 19
5. Top 5 Ball Hawks ... 23
6. Top 5 Returners ... 27
7. Top 5 Kickers ... 32
8. Top 5 Hardest Hitters ... 37
9. Top 5 Rookie Seasons ... 42
10. Top 5 Most Versatile Players ... 46
11. Top 5 Backup Quarterbacks ... 50
12. Top 5 Speedsters ... 54
13. Top 5 Fleeting Favorites ... 58
14. Top 5 Tough Guys ... 62

15.	Top 5 One and Done Seasons	66
16.	Top 5 Unsung Players	70
17.	Top 5 Did They Really Play in Denver?	75

Memorable Games   79

18.	Top 5 Super Bowl Moments	80
19.	Top 5 Craziest Finishes	85
20.	Top 5 Playoff Moments (Offense)	89
21.	Top 5 Playoff Moments (Defense)	94
22.	Top 5 Most Crushing Losses	99
23.	Top 5 Weather Games	104
24.	Top 5 Wins over the Patriots	108

Drafts, Trades, Coaches, and GMs   113

25.	Top 5 Undrafted Free Agents	114
26.	Top 5 Terrific Trades	119
27.	Top 5 Free Agent Signings (Offense)	123
28.	Top 5 Free Agent Signings (Defense)	128
29.	Top 5 Terrible Trades	133
30.	Top 5 Head Coaches	138
31.	Top 5 Head Coach Calamities	143
32.	Top 5 Late Round Steals	147
33.	Top 5 Draft Busts	152
34.	Top 5 Free Agent Flops	156

The Fun Stuff (With a Couple of Serious Categories Thrown In) 161

35.	Top 5 Comebacks	162
36.	Top 5 Celebrations	166

37. Top 5 Trick Plays	170
38. Top 5 Players with Colorado Connections	174
39. Top 5 Big Man Touchdowns	179
40. Top 5 Talkers	183
41. Top 5 Individual Player Nicknames	188
42. Top 5 Post-Football Careers	192
43. Top 5 Shocking Moments	196
44. Top 5 Feuds and Fallouts	200
45. Top 5 Famous Fans	205
46. Top 5 Group Nicknames	209
47. Top 5 Broncos Who Should Be in The Hall of Fame	213
48. Top 5 What Might Have Beens...	218
49. Top 5 Pop Culture Cameos	223
50. Top 5 Broncos Books	227
Endnotes	231
Trivia Test Answers	238
Bibiography	243
Acknowledgements	246
About the Author	247
Also By Chris Bradshaw	248

INTRODUCTION AND SELECTION CRITERIA

Down by six in the final minutes of a crucial playoff game, would you rather have John Elway or Peyton Manning under center directing that all-important drive? Tough choice, isn't it? Football is a game of opinions. Often very strong opinions.

Was Dennis Smith a harder hitter than Steve Atwater? Was Josh McDaniels the worst coach in franchise history or does Nathaniel Hackett get that unwanted crown? Was Shannon Sharpe a more flamboyant talker than Tom Jackson?

In *Denver Broncos: Top 5 of Everything*, I hope to answer those questions, plus many, many more. The book does exactly what it says in the title. I've taken 50 unique categories and tried to find the top five examples of each one.

Because the Broncos have been one of the NFL's premier franchises, there are plenty of highlights to relive including improbable comebacks, joyful Super Bowl moments, and crazy finishes. Player groups also come under scrutiny. Who are the team's top five receivers, ball hawks, speedsters, returners, rushers, and so on?

With apologies to Clint Eastwood (and Sergio Leone), while there has been plenty of good to enjoy in the history of the Broncos, there have been some bad and downright ugly times too. You'll find categories looking at the most crushing losses, the worst trades, and the biggest free agent flops, among other cringe-worthy topics.

On a more lighthearted note, there are also categories on big man touchdowns, feuds and fallouts, trick plays, celebrations, nicknames, famous fans (RIP Barrel Man), and much else besides.

Selection Criteria

The lists here are completely subjective and based on watching the Broncos for almost 40 years. They have been compiled solely from a fan's perspective.

You may well ask what qualifies someone who lives thousands of miles away (yes, I'm a Limey) to comment on the team. Well, I've been a paid-up member of Broncos Country since the mid-1980s. Let me explain.

I have a random encounter with a man from Fort Collins at York Railway Station to thank for my support of all things orange. Ten-year-old me was sporting a Colorado State University sweatshirt, which my mom had found who knows where. The mystery American was a CSU alum and was amazed to see someone sporting the logo from his alma mater in such an unlikely location. He got speaking to me and my mom and asked whether I watched the NFL (which had just started being televised in the UK). I did. "In which case," he replied, "you must support the Denver Broncos." And from that day on I've been a member of Broncos Country.

At elementary school, the class was given a task to write a letter to a famous person. While most of my classmates were penning adoring letters to Duran Duran or trying to bag a signed photo of the queen, I was writing to John Elway. I received a reply too (thanks John and Broncos PR king Jim Saccomano) and they got me for life.

Thankfully for us fans on this side of the pond, we don't have to rely on a crackly signal from the Armed Forces Radio Network to follow the action these days.

Technology means we can see all the games and hear the opinions of Broncos Country on the likes of The Fan, KOA, and Mile High Sports Radio. I don't live in Denver, but I think I've paid my dues.

Now let's get stuck in with the most important position of all, quarterback.

PLAYERS

Top 5 Quarterbacks

The Broncos have been blessed with two of the greatest quarterbacks to ever play the game. Needless to say, Messrs. Elway and Manning feature in this list of the top signal callers in franchise history. But what about the other three spots? There's room for a couple of retreads who enjoyed excellent second acts in Denver as well as an extremely rare sight – a quarterback drafted by the Broncos who actually did quite well.

5. Brian Griese

Trying to fill the enormous shoes vacated by John Elway was going to be a huge task for anyone. Especially a third-round draft pick playing in just his second season as a pro.

The man facing that rather daunting prospect was Brian Griese. The bones of the team that had won two Super Bowls in a row were starting to creak by 1999, and the former Michigan Wolverine's chances weren't helped by the ultimately career-ending injury that befell Terrell Davis in Week 4. The Broncos went from world champion to the basement of the AFC West in the space of a season. In 13 starts that year, Griese threw just 14 touchdowns as well as 14 interceptions.

Griese showed plenty of bounceback ability a year later, though, tossing 19 touchdowns and just four interceptions en route to a 7-3 starting record. A shoulder injury brought his season to a premature close, but it looked like the Broncos had found their answer at quarterback.

Alas for Broncos Country, that 2000 Pro Bowl season was as good as it got for Griese in Denver. The Broncos missed out on the playoffs in 2001 and 2002 after 8-8 and 9-7 seasons and Mike Shanahan called time on the Griese experiment, opting to roll the dice with Jake Plummer.

Griese's stats with the Broncos stack up pretty well. He had an overall record of 27-24 in Denver, and his 11,763 passing yards and 71 touchdowns are still good for fourth on the all-time franchise lists.

4. Craig Morton

Expectations weren't exactly sky-high when the Broncos signed Craig Morton in 1977. The New York Giants had gone 9-25 in the previous three years with Morton under center. That final season was especially bad. The veteran signal caller threw just nine touchdowns and 20 picks on the way to a miserable 2-10 starting record. Not numbers to get the collective pulse of Broncos Country racing.

As a former number one overall pick with Dallas, Morton obviously had talent. Was there any tread left on the 34-year-old's tires, though? Red Miller thought so, and he was proved right in spectacular style.

Rejuvenated by his relocation to Mile High country, Morton enjoyed a career year in his first season in Denver. Helped by the legendary Orange Crush defense, Morton steered the Broncos to a 12-2 record, their first playoff victory, and a maiden Super Bowl appearance.

Another division title followed a year later as well as a further postseason appearance in 1979. In six seasons with the Broncos, Morton enjoyed a 41-23 starting record and threw 74 touchdown passes, which is third on the team's all-time list.

In their early years, the Broncos weren't quite a laughingstock, but they were among the league's perennial also-rans. Thanks in large part to their veteran quarterback, the Broncos were transformed into a respected franchise.

3. Jake Plummer

Like Craig Morton, Jake Plummer arrived in Denver with plenty to prove. In six years with the Cardinals, Plummer threw 90 touchdown passes and 114 interceptions and had a starting record of 30 wins and 52 losses. Not the most impressive resume for a team looking for a big upgrade at quarterback.

Mike Shanahan took a punt on the mobile, streaky quarterback and if not quite hitting the jackpot, he certainly got plenty of bang for his buck.

With Plummer under center, the Broncos enjoyed four successive winning seasons, reached the playoffs three times, and got tantalizingly close to the Super Bowl in 2005, falling just short to the Steelers in the AFC decider.

Plummer's buccaneering style was instrumental in that run. Sure, "The Snake" could be a bit erratic, but when on his game there were few more exciting players in football.

The axe eventually fell on Plummer's Broncos career when head coach Mike Shanahan turned to first-round pick Jay Cutler late in the 2006 season. Plummer's stay in Denver was relatively short but was certainly sweet.

2. Peyton Manning

Tim Tebow was the football equivalent of a jalopy – not particularly efficient or reliable and a bit rough around the edges but a good runner that provided plenty of happy memories. When GM John Elway signed Peyton Manning, the Broncos traded in their loveable banger and upgraded to a super-smooth Rolls-Royce.

After sitting out the 2011 season following neck surgery, Manning returned to deliver a fantastic four-year run that culminated with a Super Bowl title. The numbers are pretty mind-blowing, especially the 2013 season when Manning and the Broncos rewrote the NFL record books.

"The Sheriff" passed for 5,477 yards and 55 touchdowns in 2013, both of which remain the best in the history of the NFL. The next highest number of touchdown passes in a season is 50, which shows just how spectacular Manning's annus mirabilis was. Of course, that season eventually ended up in cruel disappointment courtesy of Pete Carroll and the Seahawks.

Like fellow Hall of Famer John Elway, Manning called time on his career at the top, with a victory in the Super Bowl. Beset by injury, #18 endured the worst statistical year of his career in 2015 but, with plenty of help from an all-time great defense, had all the veteran savvy required to get the Broncos over the line when it really mattered.

In his four seasons in Denver, Manning passed for 17,112 yards and 140 touchdowns and led the Broncos to 45 regular season wins, an AFC Championship, and a Super Bowl.

A healthy Peyton Manning was a delight to watch. A true artist at the game's most difficult position.

1. John Elway

If you had to pick one player to personify the Denver Broncos franchise it would undoubtedly be John Elway. With two Super Bowl wins, five Super Bowl appearances, nine Pro Bowls, a League MVP Award, and a gold jacket from the Pro Football Hall of Fame, John Elway won pretty much everything there was to win in the NFL as a player.

Elway's stats are impressive enough, with 300 regular season touchdowns plus another 27 in the postseason. The numbers aren't as gaudy as those you'll see from present-day quarterbacks, though. The highest number of touchdowns

Elway threw in a season was 27, and he passed the 4,000-yard mark only once in his career. The numbers tell only part of the story of why Elway was so special.

In any contest in which Elway appeared, no matter how sticky the situation, the Broncos would always have a chance. In his 16 seasons in the NFL, #7 led the team to 47 fourth quarter game-winning or game-tying drives. With the score tight and the game on the line, Elway could conjure up a magical comeback from seemingly thin air.

The stats that really count as far as Elway is concerned are a hugely impressive career starting record of 148-82-1 and two Super Bowl victories.

There aren't many players who can truly sign off at the top, but Elway got the finish his amazing career deserved, winning the Super Bowl MVP Award in his final appearance as a pro.

Trivia Test

Who holds the franchise record for the most passing yards in a single game with 499?

a) John Elway

b) Peyton Manning

c) Jake Plummer

Trivia Test answers are at the back of the book, starting at page 237.

Top 5 Running Backs

It might not have the prestige it once had, but the position of running back is still a hugely important one. An elite rusher in the backfield can open up all sorts of opportunities in both the running and passing games. The Broncos have benefited from some quality rushers throughout their history. Here are the top five running backs in franchise history.

5. C. J. Anderson

He might have only broken the 1,000-yard barrier once in his career, but few backs have been as important to the success of the team as C. J. Anderson was in the mid-2010s.

The undrafted free agent was a key component of the 2015 Super Bowl championship roster, rushing for 720 yards and five touchdowns during the regular season. It was Anderson's postseason work that landed him his place on this list.

Anderson rushed for 72 yards and a fourth-quarter touchdown as the Broncos beat the Steelers in the Divisional Round playoff and then added 72 more in the AFC Championship decider against New England. The best was yet to come in the Super Bowl as Anderson rushed for a game-best 90 yards against the Panthers. He also scored the Broncos' only offensive touchdown.

Other backs have flashier stats than Anderson's, but this blue-collar back provided some great moments for Broncos Country. (See also Top Wins Over the Patriots)

4. Otis Armstrong

Who was the first Bronco to average 100 rushing yards per game over a whole season? Clinton Portis? Terrell Davis? No, that record belongs to Otis Armstrong. After starting the year at fullback, Armstrong replaced Floyd Little as the Broncos' featured rusher during the 1974 season and responded in style.

In the 14-game season, Armstrong led the NFL with 1,407 yards at an average of 5.3 yards per attempt and 100.5 yards per game. Add 38 catches for another 405 yards and a total of 12 touchdowns to that haul and you have a truly spectacular season. No wonder Armstrong was named to the Pro Bowl and received First-Team All-Pro honors.

The 1973 first-round pick never hit those dizzying heights again but was always a dangerous proposition when not bitten by the injury bug. Armstrong topped the 1,000-yard barrier in 1976 and was the leading rusher on the Broncos team that reached the Super Bowl a year later.

After a bruising eight seasons as a pro, Armstrong called time on his career in 1980 at the age of just 30. His 4,453 yards remain good for fourth place on the team's all-time career rushing list.

3. Clinton Portis

Combine a supremely talented back with the Mike Shanahan offensive scheme and you have a good chance of delivering elite performance. And Clinton Portis delivered just that. The 2002 second-round pick spent just two years in Denver but what a couple of years they were. A total of 3,099 rushing yards, 71 catches for another 678 yards, plus 31 touchdowns are remarkable numbers. There have been few better introductions to the world of professional football than that.

You might have imagined that Coach Shanahan would build his team around the former Miami Hurricane. With Shanahan's happy knack of generating quality results from all manner of backs, Portis was sacrificed to gain more defensive power. The swap deal with Washington worked out just fine for the Broncos with Champ Bailey going on to enjoy a Hall of Fame career in Denver.

Portis still delivered plenty of highlights to Broncos Country. A 5.5 yards per carry average remains the best in franchise history.

2. Floyd Little

Having a nickname like "The Franchise" tells you just how important Floyd Little was to the Broncos. The former Syracuse star broke a host of records in Denver. For starters, he was the first first-round pick selected by the Broncos to actually sign for the team. He was taken sixth overall in 1967, and the investment of that draft capital proved hugely beneficial for both team and player.

Little offered flashes of potential in his rookie season of 1967 but really started to motor a year later, earning the first of five Pro Bowl selections. By 1969, he'd become one of the AFL's top backs, averaging 81 yards per game at a very healthy lick of five yards per carry.

"The Franchise" would go on to lead the entire post-merger NFL in rushing (1,133) and total yards (1,388) in 1971. His 12 touchdowns in 1973 also topped the NFL as the Broncos made the transition from also-rans to contenders.

By the time Little retired in 1975 he'd amassed 12,173 combined yards, a total that remained a franchise record until 2006 when eventually broken by Rod Smith.

Little was inducted into the Pro Football Hall of Fame in 2010, and his #44 jersey is one of just three to be retired by the Broncos.

1. Terrell Davis

The least surprising selection in this book comes right here. Who else could be number one on the list of best backs in franchise history than Terrell Lamar Davis?

During the three-year spell from 1996 through to 1998 the stats are so ridiculous it's hard to believe they're real: 5,296 rushing yards and 49 touchdown runs in three seasons! And that was just the regular season. Throw in another 1,140 yards and 12 touchdowns from eight (eight!!) playoff games and you have one of the greatest performances in the history of the NFL.

TD has a full house when it comes to pro football honors too. League MVP, Super Bowl MVP, and member of the Pro Football Hall of Fame. He even has an appearance on *Sesame Street* on his resume (see the Top 5 Pop Culture Cameos for more on this memorable performance).

With records galore, multiple Super Bowl rings, and honors aplenty, Terrell Davis is on the Mount Rushmore of Broncos Country. Not a bad return for a sixth-round pick!

Trivia Test

Who holds the record for the most Pro Bowls by a Broncos running back?

a) Terrell Davis

b) Floyd Little

c) Clinton Portis

Top 5 Wide Receivers

The Broncos have been blessed with some supremely talented receivers. In fact, such is the number of quality catchers, this has been by far the hardest category to whittle down to just five. You'll find some glaring omissions here that could have easily appeared on another day.

5. Brandon Marshall

Brandon Marshall might not have been in Denver for long, and you won't find his name in the Top 10 for receiving yards, but for three seasons with the Broncos he was nearly unstoppable.

Picked in the fourth round of the 2006 NFL Draft, injury hindered much of Marshall's rookie season, but there were flashes of the brilliance that was to come. In the 2007, 2008, and 2009 seasons the former UCF Knight caught 102, 104, and 101 passes respectively for a combined 3,710 yards and 23 touchdowns.

Marshall's most amazing performance in Broncos colors came in a losing effort against the Colts in Week 14 of the 2009 season. Kyle Orton completed 29 passes that day with 21 of them ending up in Marshall's hands. The big receiver totaled 200 yards and two touchdowns.

So why aren't we writing up Marshall as a potential Ring of Honor or even Hall of Fame player? Undoubtedly hugely talented, Marshall also brought plenty of baggage with him. That included suspensions from the NFL for off-the-field issues as well as internal suspensions from the Broncos for "conduct detrimental to the team."

The Broncos cut ties with their supremely talented receiver in April 2010, sending him to Miami in exchange for a second-round draft pick.

Marshall bounced around the league, putting up impressive numbers wherever he went. Tellingly, he never stayed with a team for more than three seasons before moving on.

Undoubtedly a hard man to manage, Marshall is one of the most talented receivers to have appeared for the Broncos.

4. Haven Moses

One of the greatest weapons for an offense is a rapid receiver who can take the top off a defense. That type of receiver might not catch a huge number of passes, but he'll always keep the opposition honest and stop them from taking liberties. The Broncos had just such a receiver in Haven Moses.

The former Buffalo Bill had speed to burn as witnessed by an average of more than 18 yards per catch. He might never have topped the 1,000-yard barrier and only caught 50 passes in a season once, but Moses was a huge deep threat that opponents had to take very seriously every snap.

The NFL was a very different beast in the 1970s than the pass-happy league it is today. We'd love to have seen Moses get a shot in an elite offense. Imagine how he might have prospered during the Peyton Manning era in Denver.

3. Lionel Taylor

Who was the first wide receiver in pro football to catch 100 passes in a season? Jerry Rice, Steve Largent, Cris Carter? Take a bow, Lionel Taylor. An original member of the Broncos, Taylor was one of the few highlights in the early days of the franchise.

Taylor gave notice of just how special a talent he was in his first season in Denver in 1960, catching 92 passes for 1,235 yards and 12 touchdowns. He followed that a year later with a century of catches for 1,176 yards. And remember, the schedule then was made up of just 14 games.

During seven seasons with the Broncos, Taylor caught 543 passes for 6,872 yards and 44 touchdowns, leading the AFL in catches five seasons out of six from 1960 to 1966. Those stats are even more impressive when you consider how bad the Broncos were at that time. During Taylor's tenure in Denver, the team went a sorry 26-69-1. Imagine how much worse that might have been without their star receiver.

Taylor plied his trade for the entirety of his career in the AFL, which is one reason why he is often overlooked. Perhaps the most remarkable thing about Taylor is that he started his pro football career with the Chicago Bears as a linebacker.

2. Demaryius Thomas

The Broncos haven't always picked sure things in the first round of the NFL Draft. They struck gold with the 22nd pick in 2010, though, when they selected Demaryius Thomas. The first receiver taken that year would go on to have a superb career in Denver, delivering some of the most amazing moments in franchise history.

It took a while for Thomas to find his feet in the pros after an injury-plagued rookie season. The run-heavy, Tim Tebow-inspired offense wasn't exactly manna from heaven for receivers the following year either. Even so, a 2011 season that included 32 catches for 551 yards and a 17.1 yards per catch average represents some decent returns.

The former Georgia Tech Yellow Jacket really hit his stride with the arrival of Peyton Manning. In the four seasons with #18 at the quarterback controls, Thomas caught 402 passes for 5,787 yards and 41 touchdowns. The stats weren't quite as flashy post-Manning, but 209 catches from Trevor Siemian, Brock Osweiler, Paxton Lynch, and Case Keenum in the following two and a half seasons stack up pretty well. Thomas' 53 catches and six touchdowns in the postseason remain the most in franchise history too.

The numbers are impressive but it's big plays that Thomas will be remembered for. Who can forget the ridiculous one-handed touchdown grab against the Chiefs in 2012 or the 86-yard scamper against the Cardinals in 2014? And then there's the biggest one of all – the game-ending, 80-yard score to beat the Steelers in the 2011 Wild Card game.

Taken from us far, far too soon. Thanks for the memories, DT.

1. Rod Smith

Look up a receiving record in the Broncos yearbook and the chances are that it's held by Rod Smith. Career catches – tick. Receiving yards – tick. Touchdowns – tick. Smith also holds the postseason record for receiving yards and is tied with Demaryius Thomas for the most playoff touchdowns.

That's quite the return for a player who didn't even trouble the front office movers and shakers in the 1995 NFL Draft. Undrafted out of Missouri Southern, Smith was a late bloomer, entering the league at 25 and only really starting to make an impact at the age of 27.

Once he found his feet, there was no stopping Smith, who broke the 1,000-yard barrier in eight of the following nine seasons. He's the only Bronco to lead the NFL in catches after grabbing 113 receptions during the 2001 season.

A key element of a Super Bowl-winning receiving corps that included Ed McCaffrey and Shannon Sharpe, Smith was an elite receiver who has great claims to be in the Pro Football Hall of Fame.

It's hard to believe that a receiver with such hugely impressive credentials is underrated, but Rod Smith certainly is.

Trivia Test

Who holds the record for the most receptions by a Bronco in playoff games?

a) Vance Johnson

b) Rod Smith

c) Demaryius Thomas

Top 5 Pass Rushers

Pressuring the quarterback is one of the surest ways to deliver defensive success. Denver has been home to some of the fastest and nastiest sack machines in the game. Here are the Broncos' five greatest pass rushers.

5. Lyle Alzado

One of the most colorful and controversial characters to suit up for the Broncos, Lyle Alzado was a highly dangerous pass rusher on a series of dominant Denver defenses.

Selected in the fourth round of the 1971 NFL Draft, the man from tiny Yankton College made a big splash in his rookie season, racking up eight sacks and 55 tackles. That was just a taster of what was to come from the former Golden Gloves boxer. Alzado didn't miss a start from 1972 to 1975, registering 39.5 sacks in the process.

Injury ended Alzado's 1976 season after a single game, but he roared back a year later, gaining Pro Bowl and First-Team All-Pro honors as the Broncos reached their first Super Bowl. Yet more sacks (and another Pro Bowl nod) followed in 1978 in what proved to be the pass rusher's final season in Denver.

In fact, Alzado's final appearance as a Bronco at Mile High Stadium wasn't even on the football field. It was in the boxing ring against heavyweight champ Muhammad Ali in July 1979. See Top 5 Tough Guys for more on this controversial bout.

Alzado was one of the few athletes of his era to admit to using performance enhancing drugs including anabolic steroids. He died of a brain cancer in 1991, aged just 43.

4. Elvis Dumervil

Standing five-eleven and weighing 260, Elvis Dumervil wasn't the most physically imposing defender to wear Broncos orange. Long arms, great speed, and terrific technique helped the fourth-round draft pick become one of the NFL's premier pass-rushing threats.

In a stellar career in Denver, Dumervil registered 63.5 sacks and forced 16 fumbles in just 91 appearances. Only Von Miller had more multi-sack games for the Broncos than Dumervil. The 2009 season was the undoubted highlight of the former Louisville star's career. His 17 sacks topped the NFL rankings, earning him Pro Bowl and First-Team All-Pro honors as well as a third-place finish in the Defensive Player of the Year voting.

Sadly, Dumervil's career in Denver ended in a somewhat farcical manner. After agreeing to restructure his contract in 2013, Dumervil's agent faxed confirmation to Broncos HQ. Unfortunately, the fax arrived minutes after the deadline, and instead of re-signing their superstar defender, the Broncos were forced to cut him.

Dumervil spent the remaining five years of his career with the Ravens and finally the 49ers, adding another 42 sacks and two Pro Bowls to his already impressive resume.

3. DeMarcus Ware

The departure of Dumervil was a big loss to the Broncos' pass rush, but a former Cowboy would ride to the rescue a season later. The free agent signing of DeMarcus Ware was just the fillip Broncos Country needed after the Super Bowl disaster against Seattle.

With the No Fly Zone protecting the rear and Wade Phillips ready to unleash hell, Ware found a new lease on life in the Mile High City. An ideal fit for the hyper-aggressive scheme, Ware and Von Miller were a matchup nightmare for offensive coordinators throughout the league. If Von won't get you, DeMarcus will.

The pair combined for 18.5 sacks and 48 quarterback hits in the regular season before running riot in the playoffs, culminating in one of the most dominating defensive performances in the history of the Super Bowl.

2. Simon Fletcher

When assessing the NFL's most dominant pass rushers from the late '80s and early '90s, the name of Simon Fletcher is consistently overlooked. Which is strange when you look at the 11-year Bronco's hugely impressive record.

It took a while for the 1985 second-round pick to find his mojo in the NFL, but once he did he became one of the league's most consistent performers. In a five-season spell from 1989 to 1993, Fletcher registered 66 sacks, a total bettered only by Hall of Famer Reggie White.

When on a roll, Fletcher was hard to stop. He was the first man in the NFL to record a sack in 10 straight games (a record later tied by future Bronco DeMarcus Ware).

Extremely durable, Fletcher appeared in 172 straight games, the most ever by a Broncos player. Despite a high-class stat sheet that included 97.5 sacks and 20 forced fumbles, Fletcher never once made the Pro Bowl. An omission even more glaring when you consider he racked up 16 sacks during the 1992 season.

Fletcher was no fuss, all business, and one of the best pass rushers to wear orange and blue.

1. Von Miller

The four-win 2010 season was one of the worst in franchise history. The only silver lining was that it gave the Broncos the second overall pick of the 2011 NFL Draft. They used that pick wisely, selecting arguably the greatest defensive player to pull on a Broncos jersey – Von Miller.

Miller gave notice of what fans could expect right from the get-go, forcing a fumble on the first play of his 2011 NFL debut against the Raiders. There was plenty more where that came from.

The former Texas Aggie went on to register 110.5 sacks in 142 regular season games for the Broncos, adding another 6.5 in the playoffs.

The highlight of a superstar career was undoubtedly Super Bowl 50. Miller's one-man wrecking crew performance included 2.5 sacks and two forced fumbles, which was good enough for the MVP Award.

With an outlandish personality to match the big performances, Miller is one of the greatest, and most popular, players in Broncos history.

Trivia Test

B'Vsean is the unusual middle name of which Broncos pass rushing star?

a) Lyle Alzado

b) Elvis Dumervil

c) Von Miller

Top 5 Ball Hawks

When the team needs a lift, what's the best way to deliver one? A turnover. The top defensive units always seem to find a big play just when required. They may not necessarily be the best in coverage, but ball hawks can sense an opportunity and pounce. Here are five Broncos who had a real nose for the ball.

5. Justin Simmons

One of the few rays of sunshine in what's been a miserable few years for Broncos Country has been the work of Justin Simmons. The 2016 third-round pick has been "Mr. Consistency" in a Broncos secondary that has regularly been among the league's best.

A solid tackler and sturdy against the run, the former Boston College star also has an eye for the big play, recording 27 interceptions in his first seven seasons in Denver. Only one other player in the NFL (New England's J. C. Jackson) matched Simmons with four or more picks in each of the 2019, 2020, and 2021 seasons.

A three-time Second Team All-Pro and a Pro Bowler, Simmons tied for the NFL lead in 2022 after picking off six passes. After signing a lengthy contract extension in 2021, there's plenty of scope to add to that already impressive tally.

4. Steve Foley

Who is the Broncos' all-time leader in interceptions? Champ Bailey? Steve Atwater? Chris Harris Jr.? A gold star to anyone who said Steve Foley.

The former high school quarterback's route to the NFL was a curious one. Converted to defensive back while at college at Tulane, Foley's first experience as a pro was with the Jacksonville Express in the short-lived World Football League.

He signed with the Broncos in 1976, going on to play 160 games (regular season and playoffs) during an 11-year stint in Denver. Facing the likes of Dan Fouts and Terry Bradshaw could be a tricky business for defensive backs, but their gambling style also offered plenty of opportunities. And Foley took full advantage. In his Mile High career Foley registered 44 interceptions, which remains the franchise record to this day.

A starter on the Orange Crush defense that reached Super Bowl XII, Foley continued playing right up to Super Bowl XXI against the Giants.

He might not have been as flashy as others in the secondary, but he was a reliable performer on many successful Broncos teams.

3. Champ Bailey

The Broncos acquired Champ Bailey via a swap deal with Washington in 2004 (see Top 5 Terrific Trades for more), and it didn't take long for the star cornerback to make his mark, intercepting Kansas City's Trent Green in his debut appearance with the team.

After three interceptions in his maiden season in orange, the former seventh overall pick ramped things up further with eight picks a year later. You'd think that opposing quarterbacks would have gotten the message to not throw in the direction of #24, but they did in 2006 and Bailey benefited to the tune of an NFL-best 10 picks.

The interception numbers were never quite as startling in Bailey's final seven years in Denver as the penny finally dropped with opposition quarterbacks. Champ was so good in coverage that they seldom threw the ball his way. A career haul of 35 picks is still pretty handy, though.

When Bailey did get an opportunity for a pick, he often took maximum advantage, returning three of them for touchdowns.

It's a shame that the former Georgia Bulldog just missed out on the No Fly Zone era. After gaining every possible personal honor going, all that was missing from Bailey's career was a Super Bowl ring. Despite that, he's justifiably acclaimed as the best defensive back of his generation.

2. Austin "Goose" Gonsoulin

The owner of one of the greatest monikers in NFL history (see Top 5 Nicknames for more), Austin "Goose" Gonsoulin was much more than just a fancy name.

The safety broke a host of records during his time in Denver, starting with the first interception in the first-ever AFL game as the Broncos defeated the Patriots. It would be the first of many turnovers that year and in the seasons to come.

In that inaugural 1960 season, Gonsoulin topped the team and the league with 11 interceptions, a franchise record that's still intact today. The ball-hunting Goose registered 43 interceptions in just 94 games for the Broncos. That impressive total puts him just one behind all-time franchise leader Steve Foley.

A multiple AFL All-Star, Gonsoulin was inaugurated into the Broncos Ring of Fame in 1984.

1. Bill Thompson

No player in team history had a better eye for a takeaway than Bill Thompson. Drafted in 1969, Thompson spent 13 seasons with the Broncos and during that time was responsible for a franchise-record 61 turnovers.

That included 40 interceptions, which is still good for third on the team's all-time list, alongside a franchise-best 21 fumble recoveries. He put those turnovers to good use too, returning seven of them for touchdowns.

Picked by the Broncos in the third round of the 1969 AFL Draft, the versatile Thompson started his pro career at cornerback but really found his niche as a strong safety. Incredibly durable, the former Maryland State MVP started 156 straight games for the Broncos from 1971 to 1981, another franchise record.

A dangerous punt and kick returner and a longtime team captain, the ball-hawking Thompson was everything you could hope for from an aggressive defensive back.

The three-time Pro Bowler and one-time First-Team All-Pro was inducted into the Broncos Ring of Fame in 1987.

Trivia Test

Who are the two Denver defensive backs to have been voted to the Pro Bowl eight times while with the Broncos?

a) Steve Atwater and Champ Bailey

b) Steve Atwater and Louis Wright

c) Champ Bailey and Louis Wright

Top 5 Returners

There are few more exciting sights in football than a speedy return man streaking down the sideline on a punt or kickoff. Dynamic returners can be real game-changers, and the Broncos have had their share of explosive playmakers. Here are the five most dynamic returners.

5. Eddie Royal

Despite a highly promising debut NFL season (see the Top 5 Rookie Seasons), Eddie Royal never quite lived up to his potential as a receiver in Denver. He was always a dangerous returner, though, threatening to reel off a big runback from a punt or kickoff.

Royal wrote his name into the franchise record books with an explosive 2009 performance against the Chargers. The fourth-round pick returned a first-quarter kickoff 93 yards for a touchdown and then added a 71-yard punt return touchdown in the second. Royal's double was the first time a Bronco had returned a kickoff and a punt for a touchdown in the same game.

More was to come a year later as Royal returned a punt 85 yards for a score as the Broncos defeated the Raiders 38-24 at the height of Tebowmania. That would prove to be Royal's last touchdown as a Bronco.

The Virginia Tech star didn't hit the heights he sometimes threatened to in a Denver uniform, but still delivered some magnificent moments in a lean period for Broncos Country.

4. Trindon Holliday

Trindon Holliday was never likely to challenge for a position as goalkeeper on the US Men's National Soccer Team. Safe hands were not his forte. Fumbles and muffs were occupational hazards for the former LSU Tiger, but when he did manage to hold onto the ball, Holliday was one of the game's most electrifying return men.

Twice, Holliday took kickoffs 105 yards for record-setting touchdowns. He was equally dangerous as a punt returner, scoring 76- and 81-yard touchdowns against the Panthers and Giants in 2012 and 2013 respectively.

The five-foot-five returner rewrote the record books with a spectacular performance in the Broncos' ill-fated 2012 Divisional Round playoff game against the Ravens. Holliday returned a punt 90 yards for a touchdown to give the Broncos a 7-0 lead before the offense had even touched the ball. He followed that by taking the second-half kickoff 108 yards to the house for another score. We all know what happened later, though (see the Top 5 Most Crushing Losses).

You couldn't afford to drop your guard when Trindon Holliday took the field. He was the ultimate high-risk/high-reward performer.

3. Deltha O'Neal

When Deltha O'Neal got his hands on the ball, either as a defensive back or a returner, exciting things often happened. Drafted by Denver with the 15th overall pick in 2000, O'Neal gained prominence as a kick returner in his rookie season, averaging 24 yards per return and scoring his first return touchdown with an 87-yard runback against the Patriots.

O'Neal enjoyed a spectacular year in 2001, recording a team-best nine picks including four in a wild game against the Chiefs. He scored his first punt return touchdown as a pro too, taking one back 86 yards for a score against the Seahawks. Another two interception return touchdowns followed in 2002 as well as a second punt return score a year later. So potentially dangerous was O'Neal that Mike Shanahan even briefly used him as a wide receiver.

Unhappy at what he thought was a lack of playing time, O'Neal was traded to the Bengals in 2004. His stay in Denver might have been short at just four seasons, but there was plenty for the highlight reel from this explosive performer.

2. Darrien Gordon

Like Deltha O'Neal, Darrien Gordon was a defensive back who was a scoring threat whenever he touched the ball. A proper ball hawk, he touched it regularly too.

The 1997 Broncos weren't just dangerous on offense. The defense and special teams provided their share too, especially Gordon, who returned a Warren Moon pick for a 28-yard score against the Seahawks in Week 2.

The former San Diego Charger followed that up with a franchise-record 94-yard punt return touchdown against St. Louis a week later, then rewrote the NFL record books against the Panthers in Week 11. Gordon returned punts for 82 and 75 yards for a pair of scores in the first quarter as the Broncos routed the Panthers 34-0 despite scoring just one offensive touchdown.

Gordon added another interception return touchdown to his collection against Washington during the 1998 Super Bowl title run. He also had two long interception returns in the Super Bowl against Atlanta, both of which set up Denver touchdowns. His 12.46 yards per punt return remains the best in franchise history.

Gordon spent just two years in Denver, but what a couple of seasons they were, culminating in a pair of Super Bowl rings.

1. Rick Upchurch

Two touchdowns, including a 90-yarder in his NFL debut, gave notice that the Broncos had unearthed a special talent. Used largely as a running back in college, the speedy Rick Upchurch was converted by Denver into a wide receiver. It was as an explosive returner that the former Minnesota Golden Gopher made himself a household name, though.

Selected by the Broncos in the fourth round of the 1975 NFL Draft, Upchurch became one of the most dangerous return men in the history of the game, leading the NFL in 1976 with four punt return touchdowns, a record that still stands to this day.

Further honors and accolades followed including four Pro Bowl and three First-Team All-Pro selections. Upchurch was named a First-Teamer on the NFL All-Decade Team of the 1970s and Second Team on the 1980s selection. He led the league in yards per return average three times, and his career punt return average of 12.1 yards is second in franchise history.

In his nine-year NFL stint, Upchurch also bagged 267 catches for 4,369 yards and 24 touchdowns and ran for three more.

Upchurch's eight career punt return touchdowns are the most in franchise history, and his 10,081 combined yards have been topped only by Rod Smith and Floyd Little.

If the team needed a spark, Upchurch was usually the man to deliver it. He was inducted into the Ring of Fame in 2014.

Trivia Test

Which running back's 134 kickoff returns are the most in franchise history?

a) Vaughn Hebron

b) Steve Sewell

c) Gerald Willhite

Top 5 Kickers

It might not demand the level of physical perfection as other positions, but there are few more psychologically demanding roles on a professional football team than kicker. With the game on the line, has your man got the stones to convert a game-winner? The Broncos have benefited from some clutch performers. Here are the team's five best kickers.

5. Rich Karlis

If there's one thing that appears borderline insane when looking at NFL film from the 1980s it's that kickers in places as cold as Pittsburgh, New England, and, of course, Denver used to kick without wearing a shoe. The barefoot booter in Denver's case was Rich Karlis.

Signed by the team following a 478-man tryout, Karlis spent seven seasons on kickoff, field goal, and extra point duties. Very good at them he was too, becoming just the second player in franchise history to convert more than 100 field goals.

Karlis will always have a place in the hearts of Broncos fans after booting the overtime field goal against the Browns that took the Broncos to Super Bowl XXI. That Super Bowl appearance proved to be a real mixed bag as Karlis converted a then game-record 48-yarder but somehow missed from 23 yards.

After leaving Denver, Karlis had brief spells with Minnesota and Detroit and also did one-to-one kicking clinics. He didn't advise his proteges to follow his unorthodox technique, though, telling *Sports Illustrated*, "It's a lot easier to kick in adverse conditions with some tread on your foot so I encourage the kids to keep their shoes on."[1]

4. Matt Prater

The most powerful leg in franchise history belongs to Matt Prater. He gave notice of that power in just his fourth game as a pro, converting a 56-yard field goal during a 2008 visit to the Chiefs at Arrowhead.

2013 was Prater's golden year, and the stats certainly warrant a closer look. Successful on 25 of 26 field goals (96.2%), Prater set an NFL record after converting 75 PATs. The highlight of the season was an NFL-record 64-yard field goal against the Titans in Week 14. A first Pro Bowl selection followed.

The Super Bowl loss to the Seahawks at the end of that 2013 season would be Prater's last outing in Broncos colors. After falling foul of the league's substance abuse policy, he was suspended for the first four games of the 2014 season and was cut. Denver's loss was Detroit's gain as Prater enjoyed a successful second act with the Lions.

Going into the 2023 season, Prater was the most accurate field goal kicker in Broncos' history (of kickers with more than 20 attempts).

3. Jim Turner

Jim Turner's numbers don't look too special when compared to modern-day kickers. A field goal conversion percentage of 65.1% is a bit meh to 2023 eyes. But look at those numbers in comparison to his 1970s contemporaries and Turner's figures have a far more positive glow.

Acquired via a trade with the Jets (where he was part of Joe Namath's "I guarantee it" Super Bowl win), Turner spent nine seasons in Denver, scoring 742 points, which is still good for third place on the Broncos' all-time list.

Turner helped take the Broncos to two AFC West titles as well as their first Super Bowl appearance. On his retirement in 1979, the college quarterback-turned-kicker's career haul of 1,492 points was the second best in NFL history.

Mr. Reliable didn't miss a game through injury throughout his 16-season NFL career either. In 1988, he became the first kicker to be inducted into the Broncos Ring of Fame.

2. Brandon McManus

With Matt Prater suspended for the first four games of the 2014 season, the Broncos needed help at kicker. Instead of picking up a street free agent, they sent a late-round pick to the Giants to acquire Brandon McManus despite him having no regular season experience.

The rookie got off to a somewhat rocky start with the Broncos. There was even a column in the *Denver Post* headlined "Broncos must cut unreliable place-kicker Brandon McManus."[2] . It took a while to win over the boobirds, but by the following season, the former Temple grad was firmly established as the team's kicker.

McManus enjoyed a career year during the 2015 Super Bowl season, converting 30 of 35 field goals. The 24-year-old was lights out in the postseason, going a perfect 10-for-10 on field goals and 3-for-3 on extra points.

Playing at altitude certainly helps with distance, but you have to kick them straight and McManus was adept at that from long range. In 2020 he set a franchise record by converting 10 field goals of 50 yards or more.

Second only to Jason Elam on the most field goals in team history list, McManus was the last man standing from the 2015 Super Bowl-winning team.

1. Jason Elam

Spending precious draft capital like a third-round pick on a kicker is pretty rare. The Broncos did precisely that in 1993, selecting Hawaii's Jason Elam 70th overall. The bold move paid dividends as Elam became one of the most decorated players in the history of the franchise.

In his 15 seasons in Denver, Elam became a walking record book. No player has appeared in more Broncos games, nor scored more points than #1. His 152 wins are second only to John Elway's total.

Elam topped the 100-point barrier every year in Denver and scored at least one point in every Broncos game in which he appeared. Especially proficient from long distance, Elam tied Tom Dempsey's longstanding NFL-record with a 63-yard field goal against Jacksonville in October 1998. His 24 game-winning or game-tying field goals are still team records.

Voted to the AFC Pro Bowl team on three occasions, Elam is also the proud owner of two Super Bowl rings. He was elected to the Broncos Ring of Fame in 2016.

Away from the gridiron, Elam found success as a writer of thriller novels including *Blown Coverage*, *Inside Threat*, and *Monday Night Jihad*.

Trivia Test

Which kicker was cut by the Broncos despite going 15 of 16 on field goal attempts in his short spell with the club in 2014?

a) Connor Barth

b) Stephen Hauschka

c) Joe Nedney

Top 5 Hardest Hitters

Having defenders who can hit, and we mean really hit, keeps an offense honest. A quarterback gets rid of the ball a beat too early than he wants to. A receiver drops a catch on a crossing route because there's the looming presence of a noted slugger. The Broncos have had some extremely tough tacklers who made their presence felt. Here are our Top 5 Hardest Hitters.

5. Al Wilson

Linebacker Al Wilson was an extremely versatile player. Stout against the run, the 1999 first-round draft pick also had the speed to effectively patrol the middle of the field in pass coverage. He had plenty of pop too.

Taken 31st overall, Wilson proved a superb, and often rather unheralded, addition to the Broncos defense. Extremely durable, the former Tennessee Volunteer spent eight years in Denver, missing just three out of a possible 128 games.

A dominant force from the middle linebacker position, Wilson registered 723 tackles, 21.5 sacks, five interceptions, and seven fumble recoveries. It's easy to see why he landed five Pro Bowl nods as well as First-Team All-Pro honors.

There's no better example of Wilson's prowess as a hitter than in a snowy 2004 matchup against the Raiders. Facing fourth and inches, Wilson delivered a huge midair hit on Oakland's Tyrone Wheatley to stop the first down.

Often overlooked, Al Wilson was a superb servant for the Broncos.

4. Bill Romanowski

Controversy and Bill Romanowski. Words that go together like pot and kettle and flag and personal foul. When Mike Shanahan signed the former 49ers and Eagles linebacker it was certainly a gamble. It was one that paid off, though, as the Broncos won the Super Bowl in each of Romo's first two seasons in Denver.

Successful teams aren't usually made up of angelic choirboys and Romanowski was the personification of winning ugly. Sometimes very ugly indeed, as the J. J. Stokes spitting incident shows (see Top 5 Shocking Moments for more on this notorious affair).

Romo was a master of the dark arts, both verbal and physical. A potent trash talker, he had the tough tackles to back up his sharp mouth.

Regularly appearing on lists of the dirtiest players of all time, Romanowski reveled in his bad-boy reputation. Even he agrees, though, that he went over the top breaking Dave Meggett's finger at the bottom of one especially grimy pile.[3] Hated by opponents (and occasionally by home fans), Romanowski is one of the most controversial figures to suit up for the Broncos.

For all the talk and bluster, you don't appear in the NFL for 16 seasons and play in 269 regular season and postseason games if you can't play, and Romanowski certainly could.

3. John Lynch

Crunching tackles were a key part of the John Lynch resume. Even the supremely elusive Barry Sanders said that the hardest hit of his career came courtesy of the then Tampa Bay Buc.

Not even family members were exempt. Lynch once knocked brother-in-law Brian Allred out cold in a game between the Bucs and the Bears. The dominant safety brought that no-nonsense style with him to Denver to excellent effect, providing plenty of heft to a defensive backfield that also included Champ Bailey and Nick Ferguson.

Lynch spent the final four years of his career in Denver, receiving Pro Bowl recognition each season. He couldn't add a second Super Bowl ring to the one he won with Tampa, but he was the consummate professional in his time with the Broncos.

2. Dennis Smith

Only the brave or the foolhardy ventured over the middle when facing the Broncos during the 1980s and early 1990s. To complement the silky speed of Louis Wright there was the brute force of Dennis Smith, who rightly enjoyed a reputation as one of the NFL's hardest hitters.

Just ask Hall of Famer Thurman Thomas. The Buffalo rusher was knocked out cold on a short-yardage attempt in a 1990 game against the Broncos, courtesy of a hit from Smith.[4]

While physicality was undoubtedly a big part of Smith's game, it wasn't the only skill in his locker. In fact, just focusing on the hits ignores what a fine all-round player Smith was. Taken by the Broncos with the 15th overall pick of the 1981 NFL Draft (Dan Reeves' first selection, no less), Smith went on to enjoy a superb 14-year NFL career.

The former USC star's stat sheet includes 30 interceptions, 1,171 tackles, 15 sacks, 17 fumble recoveries, and two touchdowns. As well as being a defensive mainstay, Smith also excelled on special teams and was responsible for one of the most famous endings in team history courtesy of a blocked field against the Chargers in 1985 (see Top 5 Craziest Finishes).

The six-time Pro Bowler was added to the Broncos Ring of Fame in 2001.

1. Steve Atwater

You don't get a nickname as memorable as "The Smiling Assassin" unless you can deliver a big hit or two, and Steve Atwater could certainly do that. With his cheery demeanor and friendly smile, it would be easy to underestimate Atwater. Any quarterback, rusher, or receiver who did that was in for a very nasty surprise.

The first-round pick from Arkansas has a huge highlight reel but is probably best remembered for two plays in particular. Weighing in at six-foot-one and 253 pounds, Christian Okoye had a reputation as being one of the NFL's toughest running backs to tackle. When the Broncos played host to the Chiefs in the 1990 home opener, #27 gave the "Nigerian Nightmare" a welcome to remember, not just bringing him down but knocking him backwards. As Al Michaels simply put it, "Who else could do that but Atwater?" The hit came in at #83 on the NFL 100 Greatest Plays list.

As usual, Atwater was pure class when looking back on the famous Okoye hit, telling the Associated Press, "I was just fortunate to come out on the right side of that one because that guy had trucked so many people and I'm lucky I wasn't one of them."[5]

The second famous Atwater hit came on the biggest stage of all. Trying to close out Super Bowl XXXII against the Packers, Green Bay's Brett Favre was facing a third-and-six with just 36 seconds on the clock. Attempting a deep pass down the left-hand seam, Atwater delivered a brutal shot that took out intended target Robert Brooks, Broncos teammate Randy Hilliard, and himself. A play later, the Broncos were celebrating their first Super Bowl title.

Trivia Test

Who holds the franchise record for the most sacks by a Broncos defensive back?

a) Steve Atwater

b) Dennis Smith

c) Louis Wright

Top 5 Rookie Seasons

Replenishing the roster via the draft is a key component of NFL success. Better still if a new arrival can cement a starting position and deliver immediate results. Here are the five greatest rookie seasons in franchise history.

5. Bradley Chubb

Pick a player in the upper echelon of the NFL Draft and you expect instant production. That's just what the Broncos got from Bradley Chubb. Taken fifth overall, the North Carolina State pass rusher lived up to expectations during his rookie season, registering 12.0 sacks, the most ever by a Bronco in his first season. The most eye-catching performance in Chubb's rookie year was a three-sack game against the Rams, which tied Elvis Dumervil and Rulon Jones for the most sacks in a game by a Denver rookie.

Ravaged by injuries for the remainder of his time in Denver, the man known on social media as @Astronaut was a dominant presence on the defensive line when fit and firing.

After missing the majority of the 2021 season with ankle trouble, a healthy, injury-free Chubb returned with a vengeance in 2022. His stat sheet after eight games included 5.5 sacks, eight quarterback hits, and two forced fumbles. Those impressive numbers prompted Miami to send a first-round pick in Denver's direction to secure the services of the popular pass rusher.

4. Eddie Royal

Wide receiver Eddie Royal burst onto the NFL stage in spectacular style, catching nine passes for 146 yards and a touchdown in a season-opening Monday Night Football clash against the Raiders in 2008.

The second-round pick set a host of franchise records during his rookie season. His 980 yards, 91 catches, and five touchdowns remain the best numbers by a Broncos rookie. Only three receivers in NFL history—Michael Thomas, Anquan Boldin, and Jaylen Waddle—had more catches than Royal in their rookie seasons.

The former Virginia Tech grad had an eye for the national TV cameras in that rookie year, serving up his best performance in a Week 10, Thursday Night Football visit to Cleveland. Royal turned a quick slant and go into a spectacular 93-yard touchdown as the Broncos came from behind to win 34-30. His 164 yards that night were the most by a Broncos rookie.

Royal had his moments in Denver (as you'll have seen in the returners section) but never quite became the great receiver he threatened to become in his rookie season.

3. Ryan Clady

No lineman has ever been named the AP NFL Offensive Rookie of the Year. It's to left tackle Ryan Clady's credit that he got so close in 2008, finishing third behind Matt Ryan and Chris Johnson.

Needing help to shore up the line, the Broncos used the 12th overall pick in the 2008 draft to select the athletic Boise State Bronco. The move paid instant dividends for Denver as Clady went on to enjoy a sensational rookie year.

Clady, who started all 16 games, allowed just half a sack and received only three penalties throughout the whole season. That was good for Second-Team All-Pro honors.

Despite tearing a patellar tendon during an off-season basketball game in 2010, the durable tackle didn't miss a game during his first five NFL seasons.

The four-time Pro Bowler and two-time First-Team All-Pro spent seven seasons in Denver and, when healthy, was one of the most reliable players in franchise history.

2. Mike Anderson

Filling the shoes vacated by the injured Terrell Davis was a tough ask, but rookie Mike Anderson was more than up for the challenge. The University of Utah alum knew all about pressure, having spent four years with the US Marine Corps. After completing tours of duty in Somalia and Kenya, running behind a domineering Denver offensive line must have seemed a doddle.

Selected by the Broncos in the sixth round of the 2000 NFL Draft (189th overall), the tough-running Anderson ended up setting a franchise rookie record after rushing for 1,487 yards and 15 touchdowns.

Anderson delivered one of the greatest individual performances in team history in a Week 14 road win over the Saints. The 27-year-old rushed for a franchise-record 251 yards and four touchdowns as the Broncos won by a score of 38-23.

Add 195 yards against Seattle and another 187 against the Raiders and it's easy to see how Anderson became the first Bronco to win the NFL Offensive Rookie of the Year Award.

"Marine" spent four more seasons in orange and blue, signing off with a second 1,000-yard year in 2005 before finishing his NFL career with a brief spell in Baltimore.

1. Clinton Portis

The Broncos front office repeated the trick of drafting a gem of a running back two years later with the selection of Clinton Portis. If Mike Anderson was good, the 21-year-old Portis proved to be even better.

The 2002 second-round pick rushed for a rookie franchise-record 1,508 yards at a massive average of 5.5 yards per carry. Add another 33 catches for 364 yards, 15 rushing touchdowns, and two receiving TDs and you have one of the greatest rookie seasons in NFL history. Like Anderson, Portis was named NFL Offensive Rookie of the Year.

There was no sophomore slump for the former Miami Hurricane, who rushed for 1,591 yards and 14 scores in his second, and what proved to be final, season in Denver.

In desperate need of defensive help, Mike Shanahan shipped Portis to Washington in exchange for defensive superstar Champ Bailey and a second-round draft pick. With that pick Denver selected running back Tatum Bell, who himself enjoyed a 1,000-yard season in Broncos colors.

Portis enjoyed an impressive career in the nation's capital, passing the 1,250-yard mark on four occasions, but he never hit the heights he had reached in Denver.

Trivia Test

Who holds the record for the longest run by a Broncos rookie?

a) Mike Anderson

b) Clinton Portis

c) Eddie Royal

Top 5 Most Versatile Players

Having players who are adept in a variety of positions is a great asset for a coach. With more options, there are more opportunities to get creative. Versatility doesn't just count on the football field, though. Some lucky people excel at more than one sport. Here are the Top 5 Most Versatile Players.

5. Keith Traylor

A look at Keith Traylor's vital statistics heading into the 1991 NFL Draft make for interesting reading. Notably, his weight of 260 pounds. The Broncos selected the Central Oklahoma defender in the third round and played him at inside linebacker in his first two seasons in Denver. After being waived in 1993, Traylor spent time in Kansas City and Green Bay before returning to Mile High in 1997.

Was this the same Keith Traylor, though? The 260-pound linebacker had morphed into an enormous 330-pound defensive tackle. Traylor Mark II became a reliable run stuffer on the Super Bowl teams of 1997 and 1998, starting every postseason game in that period including Super Bowls XXXII and XXXIII.

Traylor is probably best remembered by Broncos Country for a classic "Big Man Touchdown." After picking off Buffalo's Todd Collins, Traylor rumbled home for a 62-yard score in a 1997 game at the Bills (see the Top 5 Weather Games and Top 5 Big Man Touchdowns).

4. John Lynch

John Elway wasn't the only Stanford grad who impressed on the baseball diamond as well as the gridiron. John Lynch was pretty handy on the mound too. So handy, in fact, that he was drafted by the Florida Marlins in the second round of the 1992 MLB Draft.

The backup quarterback turned superstar safety played two seasons of Minor League Baseball with the Marlins, etching his name in the record books as he did so. Playing for the Erie Sailors, Lynch threw the first pitch in the history of the Marlins organization. You can find his jersey at the Baseball Hall of Fame.

Lynch pitched 38.1 innings for the Sailors and Kane County Cougars, finishing with a very respectable 2.35 ERA.

Coaxed back to Stanford for a final year of college football with Bill Walsh, Lynch was drafted by the Bucs in 1993, starting what would become a Hall of Fame football career.

3. Steve Sewell

Every quarterback needs a comfort blanket. A reliable pair of hands who is always available. For John Elway, that "steady Eddie" was Steve Sewell.

Nicknamed "Versatile" at Oklahoma, Sewell could do just about everything on offense – running, receiving, and even passing. That skillset earned a first-round draft selection from the Broncos in 1985.

Drafted primarily as a rusher, Sewell earned his stripes as a receiver. In his seven seasons in Denver, the former Sooner caught 218 passes for 2,798 yards and scored 27 touchdowns.

Always a threat from the backfield, Sewell averaged more than 16 yards per catch in 1987 and 1989, which is a pretty amazing figure for a running back.

Sewell was also at the center of a number of memorable trick plays. John Elway caught his only career touchdown from a Sewell pass, and the pair also connected successfully in Super Bowl XXII against Washington.

The numbers might not leap out from the page, but Sewell was an integral part of the successful teams from the late 1980s.

2. Spencer Larsen

It's impressive enough for a sixth-round draft pick to start in their rookie season. To start on offense, defense, and special teams in the same game really is unprecedented. Spencer Larsen completed the trifecta in a November 2008 game against the Falcons.

Playing fullback on offense, Larsen helped the Broncos rush for 124 yards and two touchdowns. The former Arizona Wildcat was in the thick of the action on defense too, registering seven tackles as the Broncos came from behind to record an impressive 24-20 road win.

Larsen seemed to enjoy his extremely busy afternoon's work, telling reporters postgame, "It's a great experience and I credit the coaches for allowing me to do it. I think it's just the type of coaching staff that we have. [Shanahan] is always looking out for his players and he knew that would be fun for me. It's great for him to allow me to do that."[6]

He remains the only Broncos player to start on both offense and defense in the same game.

1. Gene Mingo

Gene Mingo's route to the pros was an unusual one. He didn't play in college, instead making a name for himself playing with a team in the Navy (not the Naval Academy's NCAA team). After leaving the service, the running back wrote a letter to Broncos GM Dean Griffing, offering his services to the fledgling AFL franchise.

A contract was agreed and so a record-breaking career began. Mingo gave notice of his all-round talents in the first-ever AFL game. The Broncos won at the Patriots thanks in part to a 76-yard punt return from Mingo, which resulted in the second touchdown in franchise history.

In five seasons with Denver, Mingo rushed for 777 yards, caught passes for 399 yards, and scored 11 touchdowns. Mr. Versatility also threw two touchdown passes of more than 50 yards and returned 34 kickoffs and 18 punts. He also became the first African American placekicker in professional football history, converting 72 field goals and 120 extra points for the Broncos.

Reliable yet also explosive, Mingo had plays of 50 yards or more as a rusher, receiver, passer, punt returner, and kicker. His 82-yard touchdown run against the Raiders in 1962 remains the longest in franchise history.

A true pioneer, Mingo was deservedly inducted into the Broncos Ring of Fame in 2014.

Trivia Test

In 2017, former Bronco John Lynch was named the general manager of which team?

a) San Francisco

b) Seattle

c) Tampa Bay

Top 5 Backup Quarterbacks

It's always important to have a spare tire in the trunk of the car. You don't really want to use it but in times of emergency, you might really need it. The same goes for backup quarterbacks. You don't expect the premium level of performance you get from a starter, but a quality backup will be steady enough to keep things moving. If you're lucky, the man from the bench can do more than manage the game and provide a spark to shake things up. Here are five of the Broncos' top backup quarterbacks.

5. Kendall Hinton

There aren't many emergency quarterbacks that feature in the Pro Football Hall of Fame. He might not have the gold jacket, but wide receiver turned signal caller Kendall Hinton was recognized in Canton after becoming the first emergency quarterback to start an NFL game in more than half a century.

Called into action after Drew Lock, Brett Rypien, Blake Bortles, and Jeff Driskell were ruled out after falling foul of Covid-19 restrictions, the former Wake Forest quarterback took the offensive reins in a November 2020 game against the Saints.

The results were about what you'd expect from an emergency quarterback. The 23-year-old went 1-for-9 for seven yards with a pair of picks as the Broncos crashed to a 31-3 home loss.

He managed to see the funny side of his history-making performance, though, tweeting, "What a blessing still unreal.. unfortunately I'll have to explain to my kids what a negative QBR is someday."[7]

4. Gus Frerotte

There aren't too many Broncos backup quarterbacks with winning records. One such example is Gus Frerotte. Called into action late in the 2000 season after an injury to starter Brian Griese, the former Washington signal caller went 4-2 as a starter and steered the team to a postseason appearance. In those six appearances, the Broncos racked up 38, 38, 38, 7, 31, and 38 points. Impressive totals for a starter, let alone a replacement summoned from the bench.

The 29-year-old amassed one of the most amazing stat sheets in team history during a wild Week 11 win over the Chargers. Frerotte went 36 for 58 for 462 yards with five touchdowns and four interceptions as the Broncos nudged past their divisional rivals by a score of 38-37. Two of those touchdown passes came in the last five minutes of a truly crazy game.

Denver's 2000 playoff run was brief, losing to the all-conquering Ravens in the Wild Card round.

Frerotte started just one more game for the Broncos before heading to Cincinnati and the Bengals starting job.

3. Gary Kubiak

Which quarterback and all-time great Bronco did Denver select in the 1983 NFL Draft? No, it wasn't John Elway (as most of you already know). The Broncos in fact used an eighth-round pick to select Gary Kubiak. It proved to be a wise move.

Kubiak's opportunities were limited with the arrival of John Elway, but the former Texas A&M signal caller became a sharp presence in the locker room and an ideal foil for his heralded teammate.

The future Broncos head coach rarely let the team down when called into playing action, enjoying a 3-2 starting record during his nine seasons with the team. That record included orchestrating three game-winning drives, most notably in a 22-19 road win over the Raiders in 1984.

Kubiak also came tantalizingly close to delivering a surprise AFC Championship win over the 1991 Bills. Replacing an injured John Elway, Kubes completed 11 of 12 passes for 136 yards and rushed for a late touchdown but couldn't quite get the Broncos over the line in a tight 10-7 loss.

The career stats might not be too flashy – 14 career TDs and 16 picks – but Gary Kubiak was exactly what you want from a backup quarterback.

2. Bubby Brister

The Broncos' 1998 Super Bowl defense started out in fine style with three big wins. The only problem, a niggling hamstring injury to John Elway. No Elway, no problem. Stepping forward? Journeyman Bubby Brister, who steered the well-oiled machine that was the Broncos offense to four consecutive wins.

The free agent pickup was more than just a game manager, throwing 10 touchdown passes and rushing for one more in his four relief appearances. The 36-year-old's passer rating of 99.0 was even better than Elway's during the 1998 season.

Brister looked to be in prime position to take the quarterback reins following John Elway's retirement a year later. Mike Shanahan instead opted to give youth a chance in the form of third-round draft pick Brian Griese. Released by the Broncos in 2000, Brister spent the final season of his 14-year career with the Vikings.

His tenure in Denver might have been short, but the Louisiana native's impact on the record-breaking 1998 Super Bowl run shouldn't be underestimated.

1. Brock Osweiler

He might have tarnished his reputation with Broncos Country by taking the money (and what epic amounts of money) and running rather than fighting for the starting quarterback job in Denver, but without Brock Osweiler, there might not have been a Super Bowl 50 win to celebrate.

The 2012 second-round pick saw limited action in his first three seasons in Denver as the Peyton Manning-led offensive powerhouse broke record after record. Called into action midway through the 2015 season after a banged-up #18 started to exhibit all the wear and tear you'd expect of a 39-year-old quarterback, Osweiler guided the team to five wins and kept them firmly in playoff contention.

The highlight of the playoff push was undoubtedly the 30-24 overtime win over Tom Brady and the Patriots.

After the Texans dangled an enormous $21 million carrot at the close of the 2015 season, Osweiler decided to try his luck in Houston rather than fill Peyton Manning's enormous shoes.

Further stops followed in Cleveland and Miami as well as another spell in Denver. None really worked out for the gangly quarterback, who called it quits on his NFL career at the age of 30.

He might not have been a Hall of Fame talent, but Osweiler was certainly a Hall of Famer when it came to business. The quarterback parlayed a career that included just 30 starts into earnings of $41 million.

Trivia Test?

Between Peyton Manning's retirement at the end of the 2015 season and the start of 2023, who was the only Broncos quarterback to register double-digit wins?

a) Teddy Bridgewater

b) Case Keenum

c) Trevor Siemian

Top 5 Speedsters

Speed. It's always been a key attribute for success in the NFL. A genuine burner on the outside can give a defense some serious headaches. Likewise, a defensive back blessed with genuine pace can use it to get out of trouble when the situation requires. The Broncos have enjoyed the services of several players who in another life might have excelled on the track rather than the football field. Here are our Top 5 Speedsters.

5. Patrick Surtain II

This name might come as something of a surprise. We know that Patrick Surtain II is superb in coverage, but a genuine burner? The former Alabama star was clocked at 4.46 in the 40-yard dash coming out of college. A good but not breathtaking time.

It was in a game against the Chargers that Surtain showed the NFL just what rockets he had. The first-round pick intercepted Justin Herbert in a December 2021 game against the Chargers and took it to the house for a 70-yard touchdown. According to NextGen Stats/Zebra Technologies, Surtain reached a speed of 22.07 mph during the return. That figure was "the fastest speed by a defensive ball carrier over the last 5 seasons."[8]

Surtain's effortless running style can trick you into thinking that he's not really motoring. When he puts the pedal down, he can really shift.

4. Louis Wright

It wasn't only on the football field that Louis Wright excelled while at San Jose State. He was pretty handy on the track too, setting records in the 100-, 220- and 440-yard dash as well as the long jump.

That blazing track speed was one of the reasons the Broncos spent a first-round draft pick on the versatile defensive back. It proved to be one of the best investments in franchise history.

Of course, pure speed on its own is no guarantee of success on the football field. Wright had football smarts in abundance too and was one of the most reliable pieces in a series of dominant Denver defenses.

"Lou-dini" played 166 games for the Broncos (plus 10 more in the postseason) in a 12 year-stint in Denver, helping the team to four division crowns and two AFC Championships. His impressive stat sheet includes 26 picks, 11 fumble recoveries, four touchdowns (see Top 5 Craziest Finishes), five Pro Bowls, and four All-Pro selections.

Inducted into the Broncos Ring of Fame in 1993, Wright certainly deserves consideration for a place in Canton.

After retiring from football, Wright stayed local, becoming a teacher in the Aurora Public School system.

3. Vance Johnson

Like Louis Wright, Vance Johnson was a tremendous multi-sport athlete in college, receiving All-American recognition in both football and track and field. Johnson won the NCAA long jump championship in 1983 and was just a quarter of an inch away from qualifying for the US team at the 1984 Olympics in Los Angeles.

Long jump's loss proved to be the Broncos' gain as Johnson became one of John Elway's favorite targets during a 10-season career in Denver. The speedy Johnson caught 415 passes for 5,695 yards and 37 touchdowns, adding another 40 receptions, 715 yards, and four touchdowns in the postseason.

While Johnson impressed on the field, his life off it was chaotic. Beset by alcohol, drug, and marital problems, Johnson spent 28 days in a coma in 2013 following an overdose. With the help of former Tampa Bay Buccaneer Randy Grimes, Johnson eventually went into rehab and got clean. Viewers can now see him on the Emmy Award-winning TV show *A&E Intervention*, helping people to overcome substance abuse.

2. Dominique Rodgers-Cromartie

Broncos Country was hoping for a big-name free agent signing after the 2012 season and at 25 letters long, names don't come much bigger than Dominique Rodgers-Cromartie.

A high school and college champion at the long jump, high jump, and triple jump, DRC clocked an impressive time of 6.89 seconds in the 60-yard dash.

The Tennessee State star raised eyebrows at the 2008 NFL Combine, registering an unofficial time of 4.28 seconds in the 40-yard dash, the fastest time by a cornerback that year. That speed, plus plenty of cover ability, prompted the Arizona Cardinals to take the defensive back with the 16th overall pick.

After three seasons in the desert and two more in Philly, Rodgers-Cromartie signed a one-year deal with the Broncos. It wasn't a bad one either. In 13 starts, DRC registered 31 tackles and three interceptions. Fans really got to see the scorching speed in a Week 8 win over Washington, where DRC picked off a Kirk Cousins pass and raced home for a 75-yard score.

The Broncos somewhat surprisingly let Rodgers-Cromartie walk after the Super Bowl XLVIII loss to the Seahawks. His replacement was Aqib Talib, so it all worked out pretty well in the end.

1. Champ Bailey

Champ Bailey had such great technique and was so smooth in coverage that it's easy to overlook just how quick he was. A superb track athlete, he excelled in the sprints and long jump as well as in the Georgia Bulldogs secondary.

That terrific track speed was on show when he set a record-breaking time of 4.28 seconds in the 40-yard dash at the 1999 NFL Combine.

Bailey took his college form into the pros, becoming one of the most dominant defensive players of the era. Able to shut down half the field, opposing quarterbacks were wary of throwing in Champ's direction.

Extremely dangerous with the ball in hand, Bailey scored three touchdowns for the Broncos, including 65- and 70-yard returns in 2005 and 2006 respectively.

Bailey was the ultimate corner, combining smarts, aggression, and blazing speed to superb effect.

Trivia Test

What was Champ Bailey's given first name?

a) Rodney

b) Roland

c) Ronald

Top 5 Fleeting Favorites

It's said that the NFL stands for "Not For Long." With a career lasting on average just three and a half years, it's easy to see why. There are plenty of examples of players who have blazed for a short period before fizzling out or moving on. Here are our top 5 Fleeting Favorites.

5. Julius Thomas

With just one catch in his first two seasons, there was little indication that Julius Thomas would become one of the most dangerous red zone threats in Broncos history. The college hoops star did just that, though, exploding into life to become one of Peyton Manning's favorite targets.

Across the 2013 and 2014 seasons, Thomas caught 108 passes for 1,277 yards. Good but not truly elite. What certainly was elite, though, was the incredible 24 touchdown catches in that period. He might not have been a great blocker, but the former fourth-round pick was virtually uncoverable at the business end of the field. The Broncos haven't had a weapon like it since.

Faced with salary cap issues, the Broncos couldn't agree on a deal with the tight end, who signed with Jacksonville. He never really hit the heights in Florida with the Jags or, later, the Dolphins. For two Pro Bowl seasons in Denver, though, Thomas was among the most dangerous tight ends in the game.

4. Brandon Lloyd

In the first seven seasons of his NFL career, Brandon Lloyd had a grand total of 2,370 receiving yards. Season eight would be different, though. Very different. Forming a fantastic connection with former Bears teammate Kyle Orton, Lloyd caught 77 passes for a total of 1,448 yards, which led not just the Broncos but the NFL. Add 11 touchdowns into the mix and it's easy to see why Pro Bowl recognition followed.

That 2010 season was a one-man highlight reel as the former 49ers fourth-round pick produced stunning catch after stunning catch.

With emerging receiving talents Demaryius Thomas and Eric Decker becoming more of a factor, Lloyd was traded to the Rams for a sixth-round pick just a year later. He'd never again pass the 1,000-yard barrier in his pro career.

The 1,448 yards in that amazing 2010 season are still good for third place on the most receiving yards in a season by a Broncos pass catcher.

3. Reuben Droughns

The Mike Shanahan-era Broncos were so good at unearthing running back talent that we could have included Tatum Bell, Selvin Young, or Olandis Gary on this list. Instead, we've gone for Reuben Droughns.

Originally selected in the third round of the 2000 NFL Draft, Droughns spent two injury-plagued years in Detroit before winding up in Denver. Primarily used as a kick returner in his first two seasons with the Broncos, the former Oregon Duck became the featured back in 2004, rushing for a career-best 1,240 yards from 275 carries.

Droughns would be one-and-done as a starter in Denver, though. In need of defensive help, the Broncos traded him to Cleveland in exchange for linemen Ebenezer Ekuban and Michael Myers.

A further 1,000-yard season followed with the Browns. Droughns also won a Super Bowl ring with the 2007 Giants.

2. Willis McGahee

After starting the 2011 season with a 1-4 record, the anemic Broncos offense needed a change of direction and coach John Fox took the nuclear option. Tim Tebow got the starting quarterback nod, and the emphasis of the offense became run, run, run.

In the 11 games that followed, the Broncos rushed for more than 150 yards on eight occasions and broke the 200-yard barrier five times. Alongside Tebow, the main beneficiary of this pound and ground approach was Willis McGahee.

The former first-round pick had already enjoyed 1,000-yard seasons with the Bills and Ravens and made it a hat trick after totaling 1,199 yards from 249 carries in his first season in Denver. Top of the bill was a superb performance in a 38-24 road win over the Raiders. McGahee accounted for 160 of the Broncos' 299 rushing yards, including 60- and 24-yard touchdowns.

The offense with Peyton Manning rather than Tebow at the controls was a rather different beast and McGahee didn't prosper quite as much. Another 733 yards was a decent enough return before he headed to Cleveland for his final NFL season.

The Tebow year produced many memorable moments, and McGahee played a big part. Which brings us to the man himself.

1. Tim Tebow

The stats are truly terrible for an NFL quarterback. A completion rate of below 48%. Just 127 yards per game. A passer rating of 72.9. Of course, those bare numbers tell only part of the story as the 2011 season was one of the most memorable in franchise history.

John Fox put his faith in Tim Tebow six games into the season, sparking an insane run of seven wins in eight games. These weren't just any old wins either. They included a crazy comeback against Miami, a road win in Kansas City where Tebow completed just two passes (one a 56-yard touchdown), and nerve-jangling overtime ass-nippers against the Bears and Chargers.

Tebow was also responsible for one of the greatest moments in franchise history. Has Mile High ever been louder than when Demaryius Thomas rumbled into the end zone for an 80-yard overtime score as the Broncos delivered a knockout Wild Card win over the Steelers?

It was never very pretty, and it required plenty of help from a stout defense (and the reliable foot of Matt Prater), but Tebow's only year as Denver's starting quarterback was a hugely exciting one.

Trivia Test

Which of the following Broncos won the Heisman Trophy?

a) John Elway

b) Tim Tebow

c) Russell Wilson

Top 5 Tough Guys

Toughness – defined by the Oxford English Dictionary as "the ability to deal with hardship or to cope in difficult situations" and "the state of being strong enough to withstand adverse conditions and rough handling." Any player who has made it all the way to an NFL roster is extremely tough. There are some players whose toughness goes above and beyond the norm. That doesn't mean they're the hardest hitters or nastiest characters, though. Toughness can be found in all sorts of unusual places. Here are the Broncos' Top 5 Tough Guys.

5. Brian Griese

One name you might not expect to find on a list of tough guys is Brian Griese. The quarterback wasn't known as a dominating physical presence after all. However, he showed the toughness of teak in a November 2000 game against the Raiders.

Griese suffered a shoulder injury after being hit by Oakland defensive back Eric Allen in the first quarter and retreated to the locker room. The verdict? A separated right shoulder. Surely that would be that for the third-year quarterback. But no. Griese was given a painkilling shot and returned to the game, despite hearing his shoulder pop in and out each time he threw a pass.

"I wasn't throwing the ball as well as I have been," Griese told reporters after the game. "Some of the balls just died. At that point, it was just your will to play, your will to win. I wasn't coming out of the game."[9]

The Broncos were grateful that he didn't as they defeated their old rival 27-24 courtesy of a Jason Elam field goal as time expired.

4. Ken Lanier

Take a look at the injury-ravaged Broncos offensive front of recent seasons and you'll see that the o-line is one of the most physically demanding positions in football. Which makes the durability of tackle Ken Lanier even more extraordinary.

Picked by the Broncos in Round 5 of the 1981 NFL Draft, Lanier was an accomplished athlete at Florida State University, setting records in the shot putt. It was on the football field that he excelled in Denver, though, appearing in 166 straight games from 1981 to 1992. That ironman streak included an offensive record 131 straight starts from Week 9 of the 1984 season through to the 1992 season finale.

Lanier didn't receive much in the way of recognition during his playing career. He was never voted to the Pro Bowl and was never named an All-Pro. He was a key protector of John Elway on the right side of the line, though, and a crucial, if often overlooked member of the Broncos teams that went to three Super Bowls.

3. Derek Wolfe

When Broncos beat writer Mike Klis asked Bill Kollar about his favorite players, the legendary defensive line coach gave two names – J. J. Watt and Derek Wolfe.[10] That's pretty impressive company for the former Broncos defensive tackle, especially given some of the names that Kollar has had under his tutelage.

Taken by the Broncos in the second round of the 2012 NFL Draft, Wolfe was the definition of a tenacious, blue-collar scrapper. He might not have had the pass-rushing flash of a Von Miller or a DeMarcus Ware, but he eked out every bit of talent he had at his disposal.

The list of injuries Wolfe suffered throughout his career makes for sobering reading. Ankle sprains, dislocated elbows, spinal cord injuries, even food poisoning. Most serious was a seizure on the team bus en route to a road game at Arrowhead. It's amazing Wolfe played as many games as he did.

When he was on the field, #95 made a big impact, especially during the 2015 Super Bowl season. A miserly run stuffer alongside Malik Jackson, the pair delivered an inside pass rush that was a perfect complement to Miller and Ware.

It's not immediately obvious from looking at the stat sheet but Wolfe gave the defensive front a gritty edge and was a key part of one of the most dominant defenses in NFL history.

And who else but Wolfe could hit the headlines after killing a 195-pound mountain lion with a bow and arrow in January 2023?

2. Lyle Alzado vs. Muhammad Ali

It's one thing to bang heads with opposing offensive linemen, but going toe-to-toe with the greatest heavyweight boxer of them all is quite another. Broncos pass rusher Lyle Alzado did just that in July 1979.

Angling for a new contract and hinting that he might swap the gridiron for the boxing ring, Alzado talked the supposedly "retired" world heavyweight champion Muhammad Ali into an eight-round exhibition contest staged at Mile High Stadium.

What was supposed to be a money-spinner for Alzado turned into an expensive cash pit as an estimated 20,000 fans paid to watch the contest, far below what promoters had hoped for.

The result of the bout was just what you'd expect, with the champ claiming an easy victory. Ali was complimentary about his plucky footballing opponent, telling the Associated Press, "For a non-fighter, he's great."[11] His contract dispute unresolved, Alzado was traded to Cleveland soon after, bringing to a close an unforgettable eight-year Broncos career.

1. Rich "Tombstone" Jackson

Every dominant defense needs to have a fear factor. Something to give the opposition nightmares. That doesn't mean being sneaky or dirty. Hard, honest, and intimidating are more than good enough, and in Rich "Tombstone" Jackson, the Broncos found all three characteristics in one domineering player.

Football in the '60s and '70s was a very different proposition than the game we know and love today. Far more rugged and much more of a physical free-for-all. Only the strong survived and Tombstone was very strong indeed.

A constant irritant to opposition quarterbacks, never was a nickname more appropriate than Jackson's. "Tombstone" spent six seasons in Denver, breaking sack and quarterback hit records as he went.

AFC West o-linemen were delighted when he moved to Cleveland. Like ironman offensive tackle Ken Lanier, Jackson was a champion shot putter at the collegiate level.

Trivia Test

Which former Bronco became a professional wrestler, entering the ring using the name "Puke"?

a) Darren Drozdov

b) Harald Hasselbach

c) Rulon Jones

Top 5 One and Done Seasons

Adding some veteran experience can be the secret sauce that turns a solid team into a contender. That experience doesn't have to be the flashy, skill position players either (although that helps of course). A bit of extra know-how can help a team get over the hump when it matters. Here are five examples of players who were in the right place at the right time and really helped the Broncos.

5. Vernon Davis

Hoping to liven up a stuttering Broncos offense midway through the 2015 season, GM John Elway turned to San Francisco's Vernon Davis. The tight end had been a consistent red zone threat for the 49ers, scoring 55 touchdowns in a 10-year spell in the Bay Area. A swap of late-round picks seemed like a steal.

Davis never quite managed to recreate his San Francisco form in Denver. A total of 20 catches for 201 yards and no touchdowns isn't a huge return. The stats tell only part of the story though. The arrival of Davis opened up plenty of opportunities for fellow tight ends Virgil Green and especially Owen Daniels (more on him below).

Speaking to the Associated Press after the 2015 AFC Championship win, Daniels said, "Having him (Davis) around, it's allowed us to do more two-tight end stuff.

To have three guys that are really interchangeable out there, he's been a great asset for us."[12]

Davis played just nine games for the Broncos before seeing out the final four years of his career in Washington.

4. Vance Walker/Antonio Smith

John Elway's bid to add more grit to the Broncos for the 2015 season meant more depth on the defensive front. He found two such pieces in Vance Walker and Antonio Smith.

The 305-pound Walker spent four seasons in Atlanta before bouncing to Oakland and then Kansas City and proved to be a handy addition to the Broncos roster. A total of 33 tackles and two sacks in the 2015 season represented a solid body of work for the former Georgia Tech Yellow Jacket.

Smith, in his 12th season in the NFL when he arrived in Denver, also had his moments during the Super Bowl run. Highlights included a pair of forced fumbles and 2.5 sacks (plus another in the Divisional Round playoff against the Steelers). The Super Bowl would be a bittersweet occasion for Smith, though, as his father died days before the big game.

Neither Walker nor Smith are household names, but they're just the sort of rotational players that are crucial to teams making a deep run into the playoffs.

Super Bowl 50 was the last game both Walker and Smith played for the Broncos.

3. Shaun Phillips

Who was the team's sack leader during the 2013 season? The obvious response would be Von Miller. However, a combination of suspension and injury meant that Miller played just nine games that season. Instead, the pass-rushing responsibilities fell largely on the shoulders of former Charger Shaun Phillips.

After hitting the free agent market, the 32-year-old signed a one-year contract in Denver and started the season with a 2.5-sack effort against the Super Bowl champion Ravens in the season opener.

The former Charger showed all his veteran savvy in a 2013 season that included 10 sacks (plus two more in the postseason), two forced fumbles, and an interception.

The Broncos couldn't quite go all the way in 2013, but Phillips played a big part in getting them quite so close to glory.

2. Evan Mathis

After being manhandled by the Seahawks in Super Bowl XLVIII and the no-show in the Divisional Round playoff loss to the Colts a year later, GM John Elway wanted to toughen the team up for 2015. It wasn't just the coaching staff that was overhauled; the o-line was too. With rookies Matt Paradis and Michael Schofield seeing significant playing time, the Broncos needed some veteran chops to help them along. They found exactly that in former Philadelphia Eagle Evan Mathis.

After contract talks stalled in Philly, the 10-year guard signed a one-year deal in Denver. It proved an ideal match for both player and team.

The man rated the top o-lineman in the game in 2013 by Pro Football Focus anchored a Denver line that while not spectacular, did enough to protect Manning and Osweiler, and deliver a more than competent running game. Mathis was "Mr. Dependable," giving up just a single holding penalty throughout the whole season.

The former Alabama lineman spent just one of his 11 years in the NFL in Denver. He won his only Super Bowl ring that year, so it worked out rather nicely for all concerned.

1. Owen Daniels

Every coach has his favorites. Players who know the system inside out and are totally reliable. In Gary Kubiak's case, that precious performer was Owen Daniels. In his 10-year career, Daniels only ever played on teams coached by Kubiak, whether that was as head coach in Houston and Denver or offensive coordinator in Baltimore.

When Kubes made his emotional return to the Mile High City, it was almost inevitable that his favorite tight end would join him. A regular season return of 46 catches and 517 yards and three touchdowns was typical of what Daniels had managed throughout his 10-year career.

It was in the playoffs, and specifically the AFC Championship Game, where Daniels would write his name into Broncos folklore. The 33-year-old scored both Denver touchdowns as the Broncos defeated New England 20-18.

A Super Bowl ring in his final NFL season (and only year in Denver) was a perfect end for the Daniels/Kubiak relationship.

Trivia Test

Which female singer performed the National Anthem at Super Bowl 50 between the Broncos and Panthers?

a) Beyonce

b) Lady Gaga

c) Miley Cyrus

Top 5 Unsung Players

In a game as tactically complicated and physically demanding as football, star power alone is no guarantee of success. Teams need depth. Players who can do the grunt work. The water carriers who set the stage for the stars to show off their magic. Here are five players who fit that bill to a tee. Unflashy and often unheralded, these kinds of guys are crucial for a team to succeed.

5. Dwayne Carswell

Nobody spends more than a decade in the National Football League without being a very good player. And Dwayne Carswell was just that. The undrafted free agent worked his way onto the roster primarily as a special teams player in 1994, but later found playing time as backup tight end behind Shannon Sharpe.

A member of the 1997 and 1998 Super Bowl-winning squads, Carswell played 163 games for Denver, catching 192 passes for 1,707 yards and 15 touchdowns.

The man known as "House" was such a physical presence and dominant blocker that he moved to guard late in his career. He still had the good hands too. In a 2005 game against the Jags, Carswell became the first eligible offensive lineman to score two touchdowns in a game.

Carswell suffered serious injuries following an auto accident in October 2005, which brought his NFL career to an end.

Two Super Bowl rings and a Pro Bowl appearance are an excellent return for the former Liberty man.

4. Greg Kragen

Six-foot-three and 260 pounds isn't the prototypical size of a run-stuffing nose tackle. That undersized physique didn't prevent Greg Kragen from enjoying a highly successful career with the Broncos, though.

An undrafted free agent signing, Kragen was one of the last cuts at his first Broncos camp in 1984. An older, wiser player with improved technique, he returned to camp a year later and made the team. The former Utah State Aggie went on to enjoy nine good years in Denver followed by four more in Kansas City and then Carolina.

Kragen played 148 games for the Broncos, providing a reliable presence in the middle of the defensive front. He could deliver the occasional big play too. While in Denver, Kragen registered 22.5 sacks and forced five fumbles. He also scored a touchdown in a 16-13 win over the Chiefs in November 1989. He's probably best remembered for an interception in the 1991 AFC Championship Game, which the Broncos eventually lost 10-7 to Buffalo.

He might not have been a household name, but the dependable Kragen more than played his part in a host of successful Broncos teams.

3. Rulon Jones

Karl Mecklenburg and Simon Fletcher were the headline attractions when it came to rushing the passer in the 1980s. They weren't the only ones who could cause panic in an opposition backfield, though. Defensive lineman Rulon Jones was very capable of creating mayhem too.

Picked by the Broncos in the second round of the 1980 NFL Draft, the six-foot-five Jones got off to a flying start in Denver, registering 11.5 sacks in his rookie season. The former Utah State Aggie took that number up to 73.5 sacks (plus six more in the postseason) during nine seasons in the Mile High City.

Jones led the team in sacks five times from 1980 to 1987, including a career-best 13.5-sack season in 1986. He currently sits fifth on the list of most sacks in franchise history and also leads the Broncos in career safeties with three.

A surprising omission from the Ring of Fame, Karl Mecklenburg thinks it's long overdue that his teammate gets some recognition.

"Rulon Jones should be there," Mecklenburg told Mile High Sports AM 1340. "Rulon was the most dominant pass rusher of his time. I made a living off of them double teaming him."[13] Who are we to argue with that?

2. David Bruton Jr.

Who was the longest-tenured player on the 2015 roster? Well done if you said David Bruton Jr. Selected by the Broncos in the fourth round of the 2009 NFL Draft, Bruton was a reliable defender, a special teams stud, and a leading presence in a locker room packed full of big personalities.

A longtime special teams captain, if there was a tackle or block to be made on punt or kickoff coverage it was usually Bruton who delivered it.

The former Notre Dame star was also an accomplished safety who gained more and more playing time as his pro career progressed. Bruton started three games during the 2015 Super Bowl season, registering two interceptions and a sack and forcing two fumbles.

A broken leg in a December 21 game against the Steelers brought that 2015 season to a premature close. Though he didn't appear in Super Bowl 50 because of the injury, Bruton was a deserving recipient of the championship ring.

After suffering multiple concussions, Bruton called time on his eight-year NFL career in 2016 at the age of 30. He remained in the Denver area post-retirement, establishing the Between The Lines Physical Therapy Center as well as running Bruton's Books, a charitable foundation aimed at getting youngsters reading.

1. Howard Griffith

If you're looking to make a splash in free agency, fullback isn't really the sexiest position to choose. Mike Shanahan made the blue-collar role a priority heading into the 1997 season, though, and hit the jackpot when former Carolina Panther Howard Griffith became available.

Terrell Davis had already led the AFC in rushing in 1996 but galloped into the stratosphere in the two seasons that followed with a big helping hand from Griffith. On Griffith's watch, Davis enjoyed 1,750- and 2,008-yard seasons as well as rushing for 1,049 yards in seven playoff appearances.

Though blocking was his bread and butter, Griffith was no slouch with the ball in hand and was a reliable receiving option out of the backfield. Never more so than in the biggest game of all. His 23-yard catch late in the fourth quarter of Super Bowl XXXII against the Packers set up what turned out to be the game-winning score.

Even better was to follow in Super Bowl XXXIII against the Falcons. Griffith scored two touchdowns on his four carries in the game.

Terrell Davis was a long overdue addition to the Hall of Fame. He owes a big debt of thanks to his reliable fullback for helping him get there.

Trivia Test

Which running back is second behind Terrell Davis with the most rushing yards for the Broncos in playoff games?

a) C. J. Anderson

b) Knowshon Moreno

c) Sammy Winder

Top 5 Did They Really Play in Denver?

A quality free agent signing can make a huge difference to a team's chances. Take DeMarcus Ware. He didn't spend long in Denver but made a massive impact. Sadly, not all big-name acquisitions work out quite as well as the former Dallas pass rusher. Here are five big stars who we sometimes have to ask: Did They Really Play in Denver?

5. Jamaal Charles

Broncos Country was very familiar with the talents of Jamaal Charles. The speedy Chiefs rusher enjoyed some spectacular performances against the Broncos, including a 259-yard, two-touchdown effort in the 2009 season finale.

The four-time Pro Bowler got the injury bug in his final two seasons in Kansas City, appearing in only eight games in 2015 and 2016. Needing a change of pace back to complement C. J. Anderson and Devontae Booker, the Broncos took a punt on the two-time All-Pro for the 2017 season.

Like many a running back turning 30, there wasn't a huge amount left in the tank when Charles rocked up in Denver. Fans were treated to the odd flash of the old speed, but 296 yards at an average of 4.3 yards per carry was way below his Kansas

City best. Add some fumbling issues into the mix and it's easy to see why Charles was one and done in Denver.

4. Leon Lett

Burly Cowboys defensive tackle Leon Lett is probably best known for his wild showboating fumble just shy of the goal line in Super Bowl XXVII against the Bills and a blocked field goal faux pas that gifted the Dolphins a win on Thanksgiving Day in 1993. Both of those plays made the Top 10 in ESPN's list of the NFL's "Top 10 Foul-Ups."

Despite those blunders, Lett was an integral part of the Dallas team that won a trio of Super Bowls in the 1990s. A dominating presence against the run, Lett got his share in the passing game too, registering 22.5 sacks, forcing six fumbles, and recovering seven more in a 10-year career with the Cowboys.

The two-time Pro Bowler hit free agency in 2001 and spent a single season with the Broncos, mostly in a rotational role. Lett's time in Denver didn't include much for the highlight reel, but he was his usual sturdy self against the run.

Lett remained in the game following his retirement as a player and has been a Cowboys defensive line coach since 2011.

3. Ty Law

Defensive back Ty Law enjoyed a fantastic NFL career. Taken by the Patriots in the first round of the 1995 NFL Draft, the speedy corner won three Super Bowl rings in New England. His impressive stat sheet includes 53 interceptions, seven forced fumbles, and seven touchdowns.

Twice the league leader in interceptions, Law was voted to five Pro Bowls, named a First-Team All-Pro twice, and was a member of the NFL's All-Decade Team of the 2000s.

Following 10 years in New England, Law had stints with the Jets and Chiefs before enjoying a final season in the pros with the Broncos.

Reunited with former Patriots coordinator Josh McDaniels in 2009, the 35-year-old Law appeared in just seven games for Denver. Broncos Country got the occasional glimpse of the old Law during that final season, including a 37-yard interception return in what turned out to be his final game as a pro. Time had caught up with the former Michigan Wolverine by the time he made it to Mile High, though.

2. Tony Dorsett

There were few bigger stars in the NFL in the late 1970s and early 1980s than Dallas Cowboys running back Tony Dorsett. Not so many people remember that the former Heisman Trophy winner spent his final year in the pros with Denver.

Looking for an upgrade to steady Sammy Winder, the Broncos sent a conditional fifth-round pick to acquire the Cowboys' all-time leading rusher.

Dorsett had rushed for just 456 yards and a single touchdown in his final year in Dallas, and the numbers weren't much better in Denver. His 703 yards at an average of 3.9 yards per rush and five touchdowns represented rather slim returns during a disappointing 8-8 1988 season.

The former second overall pick was scheduled to return for the 1989 season, but a torn ACL in preseason forced Dorsett to retire.

Elected to the Pro Football Hall of Fame in 1994, Dorsett's 12,739 career rushing yards are still good for the 10th position on the NFL's all-time list.

1. Jerry Rice

Jerry Rice never appeared in a regular season game for Denver, but the last act of his professional career played out while wearing a Broncos uniform.

Arguably the greatest player in NFL history was signed by head coach Mike Shanahan in the summer of 2005 after an underwhelming season in Seattle. The pair had a previous connection. Shanahan was the 49ers' offensive coordinator from 1992 to 1994, a three-year spell that culminated in a San Francisco Super Bowl win over the Chargers. During Shanny's stint as OC, Rice twice led the NFL in receiving yards.

The last hurrah never really worked out but was certainly worth a try. Rice caught four passes for 24 yards in the Broncos' preseason. Faced with the prospect of being fourth on the team depth chart, the 42-year-old instead called time on one of the finest careers the NFL has ever seen.

Trivia Test

Tony Dorsett threw his only career touchdown pass while playing for the Broncos. Who caught that pass?

a) Steve Sewell

b) Gerald Willhite

c) Sammy Winder

MEMORABLE GAMES

Top 5 Super Bowl Moments

It's been the scene of some soul-crushing disappointments, but the Super Bowl has given Broncos Country some monumental highs. Spectacular catches, defensive masterclasses, a mini speech, and even an eight-yard run still have the power to send shivers down the spine. Here are the team's top 5 Super Bowl Moments.

5. TD's Hat Trick

Punching it in from the 1-yard line sounds easy. As the early 2020s incarnation of the Broncos has discovered, scoring deep in opposition territory is no gimme. The all-conquering team from the late 1990s had no such problems, delivering a masterclass in red zone efficiency in Super Bowl XXXII. Hand the ball to Terrell Davis behind one of the greatest offensive lines in NFL history and watch the scoreboard keep on ticking over. Simple. The Broncos repeated the trick three times against the Packers to overcome the odds and finally win the big one.

TD tied the record for the most points in a Super Bowl, delivering an MVP performance that included 157 rushing yards at an average of 5.2 yards per carry. Those numbers are even more staggering when you consider that Davis missed the entire second quarter with a migraine (see the Comebacks chapter for more on this).

Of course, scoring a hat trick of touchdowns in the biggest game on the planet is incredibly difficult. With a Hall of Fame rusher and a superb group of blockers, the Broncos made it look effortless. And gave Broncos Country some incredible memories in the process.

4. "This One's for John"

As complex and multi-faceted as football is, there's no such thing as a one-man team. There's no equivalent to soccer's Diego Maradona, who almost single-handedly took Argentina to World Cup glory in 1986. In saying that, it's hard to think of a player who carried a franchise quite as much as John Elway did the Broncos in the 1980s. Or of someone who hauled the burden of a trio of heavy Super Bowl losses on his broad shoulders.

Redemption was the watchword for Super Bowl XXXII, and Elway found it against the Packers. The stat sheet wasn't great but all that mattered was the W. With the help of Terrell Davis, a great offensive line, and a sturdy defense, Elway was finally able to banish the demons and put away the big one.

There was no more deserving winner of a Super Bowl ring than #7. Collecting the Vince Lombardi Trophy, owner Pat Bowlen spoke for the whole of Broncos Country with the words, "This one's for John." There wasn't a dry eye in the house. In this one at least.

Elway would return the compliment after the Super Bowl 50 triumph, dedicating the victory to the memory of the late great Broncos owner: "This one's for Pat." Thanks, Mr. B.

3. Rod Smith's 80-Yard Touchdown

If the Super Bowl win over the Packers was all tension, the victory over the Falcons a year later was a rather more relaxed affair for Broncos Country.

After a Morten Andersen field goal gave Atlanta the lead, fullback Howard Griffith's one-yard touchdown run put the Broncos in front. Jason Elam increased the lead, but the Broncos really took control of the game courtesy of one of the most explosive plays in Super Bowl history.

After the Falcons missed a 37-yard field goal, the Broncos took over at their own 20-yard line. Mike Shanahan immediately went for the kill. After faking a handoff to Terrell Davis, Elway rolled right and delivered a trademark strike deep down the middle. Rod Smith caught it in stride and strolled in for a stunning 80-yard score. What could have been a 10-6 scoreline had turned into 17-3 in the space of two plays and the game was almost won.

Watch the NFL Films footage of the play and Shanahan predicts that "It's going to be wide open." And it most certainly was.

And which defensive back did Smith beat on his record-breaking score? None other than our old friend Eugene Robinson, who compared the Broncos to the worst team in the league during Super Bowl XXXII. Karma can bite back in many ways, Eugene!

2. Von's Strip-Sack TD

Given the way the Broncos defense had dominated during the 2015 season, it was only right that they scored the first touchdown of Super Bowl 50. Trailing by three after a Brandon McManus field goal, the Panthers began their second possession from their own 15-yard line. Against Denver's elite pass rush, you really don't want to be facing third-and-long, but following an incompletion and a run for no gain, the Panthers were left with precisely that.

As expected, the marauding Broncos defense teed off. Von Miller flew past right tackle Mike Remmers (a former Broncos undrafted free agent) and dragged Cam Newton to the ground for a strip sack. The subsequent fumble was recovered in the end zone by Malik Jackson for the touchdown and the Broncos were on the way.

The play was a taste of what was to come for the Panthers signal caller. Constantly under pressure, the 2015 NFL MVP was sacked six times and threw a pick in the face of the relentless Denver defense.

The top-ranked offense in the League was neutered by Von Miller and company, starting with the strip-sack touchdown.

1. The Helicopter

In a career that included countless great throws and 300 touchdown passes, it's hard to believe that the defining play of John Elway's career was an eight-yard run. But what an eight-yard run!

With the score tied at 17 with 2:16 left in the third quarter of Super Bowl XXXII, the Broncos were facing a crucial third-and-six at the Green Bay 12. Elway had been a great scrambler earlier in his career, but was there still enough life in the creaking limbs to do the job? Flushed from the pocket and with a running lane open in front of him, the 37-year-old decided to find out. After a quick glimpse at the first-down marker, Elway flung himself headfirst into three converging Green Bay defenders to gain a crucial first down. Two plays later, Terrell Davis went in for a one-yard score and the Broncos were in control again.

The play had a huge Impact not just on the scoreboard but on Elway's teammates.

Speaking to *Sports Illustrated* after the game, Shannon Sharpe said, "When I saw him do that and then get up pumping his fist, I said, 'It's on.' That's when I was sure we were going to win."[14]

"The Helicopter" was voted #33 in the NFL's 100 Greatest Plays of All-Time.

Trivia Test

Which defensive back registered Denver's only interception at Super Bowl 50 against the Panthers?

a) Chris Harris Jr.

b) Aqib Talib

c) T. J. Ward

Top 5 Craziest Finishes

It's never wise to leave a game early. So what if you beat the traffic by half an hour? In those extra minutes coasting on the freeway, you might have missed something truly spectacular on the field. Like these examples of crazy Broncos finishes.

5. If at First You Don't Succeed...

The Broncos were staring a costly fourth defeat of the 1985 season in the face in a Week 11 clash against San Diego. With the score tied at 24 five minutes into overtime, the Chargers had the ball at the Denver 23-yard line and were about to try a game-winning 40-yard field goal.

Step forward Dennis Smith. The hard-hitting safety had already blocked a Bob Thomas field goal in the first quarter and repeated the trick in overtime. To the despair of Broncos Country, though, special teams skipper Mike Harden had called a timeout just before the try, giving San Diego a second shot to win.

No problem. Smith burst through the line once again to record another block, which was scooped up by Louis Wright, who waltzed into the end zone for a 60-yard score to give the Broncos an amazing victory. Cue an amazing eruption of noise at Mile High Stadium.

The win was just the fourth time in NFL history that a team had won in overtime without their offense touching the ball.

4. Birth of Tebowmania

The 1-4 Broncos trailed Miami 15-0 deep in the fourth quarter of their 2011, Week 7 encounter at Hard Rock Stadium. The offense had shown virtually nothing in the game's first 55 minutes. Quarterback Tim Tebow had completed just four passes and the team was a pathetic 0—for-10 on third down. Defeat looked inevitable.

Starting at their own 20 with just over five minutes on the clock, Tebow orchestrated an eight-play, 80-yard drive that culminated in a Demaryius Thomas touchdown. Matt Prater's onside kick was collected by Virgil Green, and the Broncos had hope.

Ten plays later and with just 25 clicks left on the clock, Tebow completed a second touchdown pass, this time to Daniel Fells, to bring the deficit down to two. A successful two-point conversion followed, and we were heading to overtime.

The home side got the ball first, but a D. J. Williams sack and a Matt Moore fumble gave Denver possession in Miami territory. Three plays later, Prater booted the game-winning 52-yard field goal for the unlikeliest of wins.

Following the Miami Miracle, the Broncos would go on to win six of their next seven games, setting up a wild playoff run. Tebowmania was up and running.

3. Blocked PAT to Win

A road loss to the Saints looked inevitable late in the Broncos' Week 10 visit to the Superdome in 2016 after Drew Brees tossed a 32-yard touchdown pass to Brandin Cooks with 1:22 left on the clock to tie the scores at 23 apiece. All New Orleans needed was reliable kicker Will Lutz to convert the extra point. Simple.

Needing a missed kick to likely take the game to overtime, the Broncos did even better, and in the process secured one of the most extraordinary wins in franchise history.

A soaring Justin Simmons leapt over the line to block the PAT. Fellow rookie Will Parks collected the ball and scampered up the sideline for a two-point score to silence a stunned home crowd. The Broncos recovered the subsequent Saints onside kick to claim an improbable 25-23 victory.

2. 2015 Kansas City Miracle

There are few better examples of the ball-hawking Wade Phillips defense than the knockout comeback win against the Chiefs in Week 2 of the 2015 season.

Down seven with just 36 seconds on the clock, Peyton Manning found Emmanuel Sanders for the game-tying score. Overtime, here we come. Not so fast, though. With just 27 seconds left, linebacker Brandon Marshall forced a fumble from Chiefs running back Jamaal Charles, which was gratefully scooped up by Bradley Roby, who returned it 21 yards for the game-winning touchdown.

The Broncos tied an NFL record in the process with that amazing comeback victory, recording their 13th straight road win against divisional opponents. It was also a sign of what was to come from this defensive powerhouse for the remainder of the season.

1. Immaculate Deflection

The 2009 season opener at Cincinnati hadn't exactly been a classic. Two sputtering offenses had combined to score just 13 points with the Broncos, deep in their own territory, trailing 7-6 with just 28 seconds remaining.

Needing something miraculous, quarterback Kyle Orton heaved a final hopeful ball up the left sideline to a triple-covered Brandon Marshall. Cincy DB Leon Hall batted the pass as his two fellow defensive backs crashed into each other. The ball dropped into the hands of the only other body in the area, Brandon Stokley, who ran it into the end zone for the 87-yard touchdown.

"I just remember seeing the ball up in the air," Stokley told DenverBroncos.com. "And then just kind of being in disbelief that once I caught it, that nobody was there to tackle me that late in the game. Then after that, it was pretty much a blur. Just kind of 'Please don't get caught' type of thinking."[15]

The play, dubbed the Immaculate Deflection, was the longest game-winning touchdown in the final minute of the final quarter of a game.

Trivia Test

Former Broncos receiver Brandon Stokley spent the first four seasons of his NFL career with which team?

a) Baltimore

b) Indianapolis

c) Seattle

Top 5 Playoff Moments (Offense)

When it comes to playoff drama (good and bad) few teams can match the Broncos. With wild comebacks, tension-packed finales, and crazy endings, Broncos Country has seen it all. Here are the five greatest playoff moments from the offensive side of the ball.

5. TD's 199 Yards

The Broncos were the dominant team in the AFC in 1998, starting the season with 13 straight wins. There was a bit of a wobble as the postseason approached, though, courtesy of back-to-back losses to the Giants and Dolphins.

There couldn't be a repeat of the Jacksonville debacle from two years before when the playoffs began? Absolutely not. Mike Shanahan's men got their revenge on the upstart Dolphins in the Divisional Round playoff, delivering one of the most clinical all-round performances in team history.

The defense intercepted Dan Marino twice and held Miami to just 14 rushing yards, and John Elway was neat and efficient. The undoubted star of the show, though, was Terrell Davis, who rushed for 199 yards from just 21 carries. TD's two touchdowns in the first quarter gave the Broncos a 14-0 lead, which they eventually extended to a franchise-best 38-3 scoreline thanks to further touchdowns from Derek Loville, Rod Smith, and defensive lineman Neil Smith.

Davis' 199 rushing yards was the best by a Broncos back in a playoff game. In fact, only three backs in NFL history had rushed for more in a postseason game.

After the late-season jitters, the super-efficient Broncos bandwagon was back on track and ready for another Super Bowl.

4. Morton to Moses

After gaining their first-ever postseason win against the Steelers a week earlier, the Broncos faced old enemy Oakland on New Year's Day 1978 with a place in Super Bowl XII up for grabs.

The defending Super Bowl-champion Raiders edged in front with an early field goal, but a 74-yard touchdown connection from Craig Morton to Haven Moses gave the Broncos the lead, a lead they would hold for the rest of the contest.

With the suffocating Orange Crush defense living up to its name by restricting the Raiders to 94 rushing yards at an average of just 2.6 yards per carry, the Broncos were always in control.

The MVP for Denver was Moses, whose stat line for the day included five catches for 168 yards and a 33.6 yards per catch average. Add a 12-yard touchdown reception in the fourth quarter to his 74-yarder in the first and it was a performance for the ages.

A Dave Casper touchdown gave the Raiders hope late in the fourth quarter, but the Broncos ran out the final three minutes to send the Mile High crowd into ecstasy and the team to their first Super Bowl appearance.

3. Elway to Sharpe

Consider all the explosive touchdowns the Broncos have scored throughout their playoff history. Sometimes, a rather humbler 18-yard gain for a first down can be just as crucial. That was exactly what Shannon Sharpe delivered in the 1997 AFC

Championship win over the Steelers. And better still, the play wasn't even in that week's game plan.

The Broncos led 24-14 heading into the fourth quarter, but a Kordell Stewart to Charles Johnson touchdown made it a three-point game with less than three minutes on the clock. Pinned on the 11-yard line from the subsequent kickoff, Denver needed a first down to eat the clock and virtually ice the game. A three-and-out was definitely not what was required, but facing a third-and-six from their own 15, they were staring that ugly situation in the face. Don't make those six yards and even with a decent punt the Steelers would be close to field goal range.

It didn't come to that thanks to a memorable connection between John Elway and Shannon Sharpe. Elway's instruction in the huddle consisted of "just get open," and the Hall of Fame tight end did exactly what his quarterback asked of him, grabbing an 18-yard reception for a crucial first down. An Ed McCaffrey catch and two Terrell Davis runs later and the Broncos were on their way to a date with destiny with the Green Bay Packers.

2. Tebow to Thomas

"Here we go. First snap of overtime. The Broncos have been in three overtime games this year and won them all." So began Jim Nantz's commentary as Tim Tebow took the ball with the score tied at 23 in the 2011 Wild Card game against Pittsburgh. It wouldn't take long for them to take that overtime win tally to four – 11 seconds to be exact.

Tebow threw a crosser over the middle. Demaryius Thomas caught it in stride and raced down the sideline toward the end zone. Steelers defensive back Ike Taylor had a shot at making a tackle, but a couple of stiff-arms later DT was in the end zone, celebrating one of the most memorable plays ever seen at Mile High.

The walk-off touchdown was a record-breaker. It was the longest play to decide a postseason overtime game and also the fastest overtime win in playoff football.

The 80-yard touchdown was the culmination of a superb night for Thomas, who caught four passes for 204 yards.

The play came in at #76 in NFL Films' 100 Greatest Plays of All Time.

The Tebow bubble burst in New England a week later, but the Thomas touchdown was a perfect pinnacle to what had been an amazing season.

1. The Drive – Elway to Jackson

Broncos Country had seen glimpses of just what John Elway was capable of in his first three seasons in Denver. He truly came of age in season four, though, leading the Broncos to an AFC West title and a deep playoff run.

Nothing exemplifies that coming of age better than the closing stages of the AFC Championship Game against Cleveland and the series known simply as "The Drive."

Trailing by seven in the closing stages of the fourth quarter and backed up at their own 2-yard line, Elway orchestrated a 15-play drive. Passes to Steve Sewell, Steve Watson, and Mark Jackson plus some timely scrambling put the Broncos in striking distance for the game-tying score. With the ball at the Cleveland 5-yard line, Elway threw a strike to Jackson for the touchdown. After 98 yards, five minutes, and two seconds, a legend was born.

More Elway magic followed in overtime. 22 and 28-yard passes took the Broncos from their own 25 deep into Cleveland territory. Rich Karlis sealed the deal with a 33-yard field goal and the Broncos were heading to their second Super Bowl.

Trivia Test

Owen Daniels is one of two Broncos tight ends to score two touchdowns in a single playoff game. Who is the other?

a) Clarence Kay

b) Shannon Sharpe

c) Julius Thomas

Top 5 Playoff Moments (Defense)

Playoff games are arguably even more tense for the fans than the Super Bowl. Win and you're in. Lose and a whole season's work can disappear faster than an Earnest Byner fumble. Broncos Country has been treated to some spectacular postseason action from the defense. Here are our Top 5 Playoff Moments from that side of the ball.

5. Darrien Gordon vs Chiefs

Darrien Gordon's time in Denver was brief. The former Charger spent just two years with the Broncos, but there was plenty of spectacular action to enjoy in that period. Probably best known as an explosive punt returner (he scored three punt return touchdowns in 1997 alone), Gordon also impressed at right cornerback in the team's two 1990s Super Bowl triumphs.

A real ball hawk, Gordon picked off four passes in both the 1997 and 1998 regular seasons. The former Stanford star also excelled in the postseason, logging a franchise-record five interceptions in just seven playoff games for the Broncos.

The play I've chosen here certainly isn't the most explosive in the Gordon scrapbook. It's arguably the most important, though.

Trailing 14-10 at Arrowhead in the 1997 AFC Divisional Round playoff, the Chiefs had one final shot at stealing a victory. Facing fourth-and-two at the Denver 20-yard line with just 19 seconds on the clock, Kansas City quarterback Elvis Grbac lobbed a potential game-winning pass toward Lake Dawson. A perfectly positioned Gordon got the tip, the pass fell incomplete, and the Broncos were on their way to Pittsburgh for the AFC Championship.

4. Tom Jackson vs. the Steelers

The Broncos made a huge impression during the 1977 regular season, compiling a franchise-best 12-2 record. Could they bring home the bacon when the season was on the line in the playoffs, though? The team hadn't even appeared in a playoff game throughout their history, after all.

If Terry Bradshaw and the visiting Pittsburgh Steelers were expecting an easy ride, they would be rudely awakened by a dominant Denver defense and a raucous Mile High crowd.

Central to much of the best the Broncos had to offer on that chilly Christmas Eve day was Tom Jackson. The star linebacker recovered a second quarter fumble to set up a touchdown and then intercepted a pass in the fourth to set up another three points. With the Steelers trailing 24-21 in the fourth quarter, Jackson repeated the trick, grabbing his second pick to put the Broncos firmly in the driving seat.

A Craig Morton to Jack Dolbin touchdown in the closing moments sealed the 34-21 victory and prevented the Steelers from reaching a fourth straight AFC Championship Game.

If anyone thought the upstart Broncos season had been a fluke, Tom Jackson's efforts made them think otherwise.

3. Champ's 100-Yard Pick

With apologies to Tom Coughlin and the New York Giants, the one team that consistently caused headaches for Tom Brady was the Denver Broncos. Brady had a winning record against every team in the league bar the 49ers and Broncos.

One such example of the Broncos' kryptonite-like qualities came in a memorable 2005 AFC Divisional Round playoff game. A sturdy Denver defense held the explosive Patriots offense to just a single touchdown during a 27-14 win.

The game is best known for one play in particular. Trailing 10-6, the Patriots had worked their way to the Denver 5-yard line and a potential go-ahead score. Facing a third-and-five, Brady, under severe pressure from blitzing safety Nick Ferguson, tossed a hopeful pass to Troy Brown in the end zone. Champ Bailey read it beautifully, swooped in for the pick, and danced 100 yards down the sideline before being pushed out of bounds at the Patriots 1-yard line. Mike Anderson punched it in one play later to give the Broncos a 17-6 lead and a huge swing.

Surprisingly, that was Champ's only playoff interception as a Bronco. It remains the longest interception return in postseason history that didn't result in a touchdown.

2. No You Don't, Tom

Tom Brady had more reasons to be sick of visiting the Mile High City following the 2015 AFC Championship decider. The Broncos held the lead from the middle of the first quarter, but a Rob Gronkowski touchdown with just 12 seconds on the clock made the score 20-18. A successful two-point conversion and a seemingly unlosable game would be heading to overtime.

Brady took the shotgun snap and rolled right, Gronkowski again the most obvious target. Instead, Brady looked to the middle of the end zone and Julian Edelman. Malik Jackson and Aqib Talib read the play perfectly, with the latter getting the crucial tip. The ball floated into the hands of Bradley Roby, the Patriots were cooked, and the Broncos were on their way to Super Bowl 50.

Yes, it's technically a special teams play, but it was the defense that did the business once again.

1. The Fumble

You have to feel a bit sorry for poor Marty Schottenheimer. After "The Drive" a year earlier, the Cleveland coach was on the receiving end of yet more heartache from the Broncos courtesy of "The Fumble" (and the there'd be more to come two years later and with the Chiefs in the following decade).

Leading 21-3 at the half and 28-10 early in the third quarter of the 1987 AFC Championship Game, the Broncos looked to be coasting toward a second successive Super Bowl appearance. The visitors scored 21 of the next 24 points, though, to tie the game at 31. Sammy Winder's 20-yard touchdown catch late in the fourth quarter nudged the Broncos ahead, but Bernie Kosar drove the visitors deep into Denver territory with less than two minutes on the clock.

"These are the toughest yards in football," said a prophetic Merlin Olsen on commentary just before the second-and-five play from the Denver 8-yard line. Kosar handed the ball to Earnest Byner, who had already scored twice that day. The hat trick looked a certainty as Byner swept left for the game-tying score. Broncos cornerback Jeremiah Castille had other ideas, though, stripping the ball and then recovering the fumble.

Denver took a late safety as they ran out the clock, executing a Houdini-like escape courtesy of the opportunistic play of Castille.

"The Fumble" came in at #49 on the NFL's 100 Greatest Plays of All Time.

Trivia Test

Who holds the franchise record for the most sacks in postseason games?

a) Simon Fletcher

b) Karl Mecklenburg

c) Von Miller

Top 5 Most Crushing Losses

"The greater danger for most of us lies not in setting our aim too high and falling short, but in setting our aim too low and achieving our mark." So said the great Renaissance era painter Michelangelo.

The peril in that, of course, is that if you do get close to the big one but fall short, the disappointment can be devastating. Let's face it, Broncos fans have suffered more than their share of heartache at the Super Bowl. At least if you reach the Super Bowl, there's been an AFC championship to celebrate. The regular season and the playoffs have delivered some knockout blows too. Here are the Top 5 Most Crushing Losses.

5. Raiders 59, Broncos 14

Losing to the Raiders is always bad. Losing to them at home is even worse. Being totally embarrassed by them at Mile High is a potential firing offense.

The wheels hadn't quite fallen off the Josh McDaniels wagon, but they were definitely starting to wobble by the middle of the 2010 season. The Broncos had lost eight of their final 10 games in 2009 and were a miserable 2-4 as the Raiders rode into town. Needing a win over their biggest rival to keep their season alive, the Broncos served up one of the worst performances in franchise history.

Less than halfway through the second quarter, the Broncos were 38-0 down. Let's write that again – 38-0 down at home in the second quarter. This wasn't just a rout, it was a total humiliation from a team that had come into the game with the same 2-4 record as the Broncos.

The visitors rushed for 328 yards and five touchdowns and Jason Campbell threw two more as the Raiders won by a score of 59-14. And that was without any points in the fourth quarter.

Five defeats in the following six games brought the McDaniels experiment in Denver to a premature and welcome end. The only bright spot from that sorry season was receiving the No. 2 draft pick, which the Broncos would use on a rather handy pass rusher.

4. 1996 vs. Jaguars

The 1996 Broncos had enjoyed a terrific regular season. With a top five offense and a top ten defense, Denver had the look of a championship-caliber team. Unbeaten at home while compiling a 13-3 record and holding the No. 1 seed, the Broncos welcomed the upstart Jacksonville Jaguars, in only their second NFL season, to Mile High for the Divisional Round playoff game.

The game seemed to be following the predicted script as the Broncos scored the game's first two touchdowns to take a 12-0 lead. There were signs of sloppiness, though, as the first PAT was blocked, and the two-point conversion failed.

Then it all went wrong. The Jags scored on five straight possessions to take a 23-12 fourth-quarter lead. Trailing 30-20 with less than two minutes left, Elway found Ed McCaffrey to make it a three-point game. The Jags recovered the onside kick to seal one of the biggest upsets in playoff history.

Shannon Sharpe spoke for pretty much all of Broncos Country after the game when he said, "I'm just going to go home, sit on my couch, and probably cry."[16]

The Broncos would get their revenge over the Jags a year later, but this one still hurts.

3. Double OT Disaster vs. Ravens

On the back of a superb first season from Peyton Manning, the Broncos raced into the playoffs with a 13-3 record and home field advantage. First up were the Baltimore Ravens, a team the Broncos had comfortably beaten on the road less than a month previously.

In a game filled with explosive plays including punt and kickoff return touchdowns from Trindon Holliday, the game is best remembered for a monumental mess-up in the closing stages.

With the Broncos leading 35-28 and just 31 seconds on the clock, the Ravens needed a miracle. They found it in the form of a busted coverage in the Denver secondary as Joe Flacco connected with Jacoby Jones from 70 yards to take the game to overtime.

A second pick of the night from Peyton Manning in the closing stages of the first period of overtime gave the Ravens the ball in Denver territory. The visitors drove into field goal range at the start of the second period of overtime and rookie Justin Tucker duly obliged with the game-winning 47-yard kick.

Speaking after the game, future Broncos quarterback Joe Flacco admitted that the Ravens had ridden their luck. "You have to get a bit lucky. It worked out and we were able to take a shot, and everybody came through and when that opportunity arose, there is no way to explain it. It was an awesome football game. It was just crazy."[17] It most certainly was.

2. New Jersey Nightmare

The 2013 Broncos were an offensive juggernaut and an absolute delight to watch. Led by a rampant Peyton Manning and his 55 touchdown passes, they became the first team in NFL history to score more than 600 points in a season.

After seeing off the Chargers and Patriots in the Divisional and Championship rounds, the final challenge waiting the Broncos was Seattle and its top-ranked defense.

John Fox's team went into the game as a slight favorite but got a huge wakeup call from the first play from scrimmage. Manny Ramirez's snap sailed over Peyton Manning's head and the Seahawks were on the board with a safety.

The Broncos held Seattle to a pair of Stephen Haushka field goals in the remainder of the first quarter to keep things close. Things quickly fell apart, though. Marshall Lynch scored from a yard out and Malcolm Smith returned a Manning interception 69 yards for a score. To add salt to an already gaping wound, the Seahawks opened the second half by returning the kickoff for an 87-yard touchdown.

Demaryius Thomas grabbed a consolation TD, but the 43-8 final score was a true reflection on what had been a right hammering.

Outbattled, outprepared, outmuscled, and outcoached, GM John Elway realized things needed to change in a big way. Out went the explosive offense. In came Ware, Talib, Ward, and Stewart, and within two years the Broncos were celebrating again.

1. Washington 42-10 over Denver

All five of the team's Super Bowl losses were crushers. The one against Washington hurt the most, though. This was a matchup that was eminently winnable.

The game couldn't have gotten off to a better start thanks to a 56-yard John Elway to Ricky Nattiel bomb on the Broncos' first play from scrimmage. Tag on a Rich Karlis field goal and a 10-0 lead at the end of the first quarter looked pretty fine and dandy.

That was as good as it got for Dan Reeves' men as the Broncos gave up a Super Bowl-record 35 points in the second quarter. There would be no second-half heroics as Washington eventually cantered home 42-10.

The defense gave up over 600 yards and had no answer to unheralded Timmy Smith, who ran for a record 204 yards from just 22 carries.

The warning signs had been there in the AFC Championship decider against Cleveland. The Broncos conceded 30 second-half points and just hung on to win 38-33.

After going into the game as a 3.5-point favorite, this capitulation was a massive letdown.

Trivia Test

In November 2013, the Broncos tied an unwanted franchise record after blowing a 24-point lead against which opponent?

a) New England Patriots

b) Oakland Raiders

c) Seattle Seahawks

Top 5 Weather Games

A bright fall day with a temperature of about 65 are just about the perfect conditions for a Broncos home game. Of course, the vagaries of the Colorado climate mean that it's possible to experience all four seasons during a single quarter of play. Here are some of the wildest weather conditions in which the Broncos have played.

5. Don't Forget the Sunscreen – On the Road in Arizona

The weather in Colorado can have you reaching for the sun lotion early in the season, but it's nothing compared to the temperatures in Arizona. The only time the Broncos have played a game where the mercury has topped the 100-degree mark was a 2001 clash against the Cardinals.

Played in sweltering temperatures that reached a high of 103, the Broncos fell behind 10-0 early in the second quarter. On the back of one of Brian Griese's best performances as a Bronco, the visitors rallied, scoring 38 unanswered points to eventually win the game 38-17.

The game was also one of Rod Smith's best. An uncoverable #80 caught 14 passes for 162 yards and two touchdowns. Another curio of this one-sided encounter was the home team's quarterback – Jake Plummer. The Snake would play one more season in the desert before signing with Denver and becoming one of the top five Broncos signal callers of all time. Also appearing for the Cardinals that day was Corey Chavous, nephew of longtime Broncos pass rusher Barney Chavous.

4. Don't Forget Your Thermals

The coldest game to feature the Broncos was a frigid December 1983 road trip to Kansas City. There wasn't much in the way of Christmas cheer on show at Arrowhead as the Broncos crashed to a heavy defeat with temperatures dropping to zero with a wind chill of minus-30.

A Rich Karlis field goal (not really a day for a barefoot kicker) was all Denver could muster in the first three quarters as the hosts ran up a massive 41-3 lead. A miserable John Elway completed just 13 passes and threw four interceptions in one of the more forgettable outings of his rookie season. Gerald Willhite rushed for a couple of fourth-quarter touchdowns to give the score a bit more respectability, but it was still a rout.

Despite the loss in this season finale, the 9-7 Broncos just snuck into the playoffs. The postseason came to an ugly end a week later as the team lost 31-7 to division rival Seattle in the Wild Card round.

3. Let It Snow, Let It Snow, Let It Snow

In any game at Mile High, there's a chance that snow can roll in from the Rockies and really liven up proceedings. And boy did it liven up proceedings in an October 1984 game against Green Bay. More than a foot of snow dropped during the game that became known as the "Bronco Blizzard."

If there was one team (other than the Broncos) that you might expect to cope perfectly well with wintry conditions, it was the Packers. Two fumbles from their first two offensive plays, which were returned for touchdowns by Steve Foley and Louis Wright, suggested otherwise.

Green Bay scored twice in the second half, but the Broncos held on to take the game 17-14 in front of a hardy crowd of more than 62,000. The matchup was the 200th to be shown on Monday Night Football and, thanks in part to the memorable conditions, attracted record viewing figures.

2. Snowball Game

The Broncos welcomed the San Francisco 49ers to Mile High in November 1985, once again on Monday Night Football. Despite heavy snow in the run-up to the game, the field had been cleared and was ready for action.

The stadium crew hadn't managed to do the same to the stands, though, and that would become a factor just before halftime. With the Broncos leading 14-3 courtesy of John Elway touchdown passes to Gene Lang and Steve Watson, the 49ers had a chance to reduce the deficit with a 19-yard field goal.

What should have been a chip shot went badly awry thanks to a well-directed snowball from the stands. Landing just in front of holder Matt Cavanaugh it caused just enough of a distraction to put him off his hold. Instead, he attempted a pass, which fell incomplete, and the Broncos preserved their 11-point lead heading into the break. The miss would prove crucial as the home side hung on to win the game 17-16.

Speaking after the game, referee Jim Tunney said, "We have no recourse in terms of a foul or to call it on the home team or the fans. There's nothing in the rulebook that allows us to do that."[18]

1. Buffalo Stance

The weather report for the Broncos' 1997 visit to Buffalo looked like just what you'd expect from an October trip to upstate New York. A not exactly tropical 35 degrees, 11 mph winds, and a wind chill of 30. The reason this game makes it into the top five weather games comes from the atrocious conditions at the start of this Week 9 road trip.

A huge blizzard dumped almost two feet of snow on the Denver area the night before the team's charter was due to fly. The ride from the team facility to the airport usually took 30 minutes. Instead, it took two and a half hours. With the help of sleds, snowplows, and the Colorado State Patrol, all the players and staff somehow made it.

The charter took off 10 hours late and touched down in Buffalo in the early hours of Sunday morning. That late arrival left precious little preparation time for the contest against the 4-3 Bills. No preparation, no problem.

Mike Shanahan's Broncos were such a well-oiled machine that they were up 20-0 heading into the fourth quarter. Things got a little hairy as the Bills mounted a terrific comeback with Steve Christie tying the score at 20 with a minute to go. Jason Elam saved the day, though, booting a 33-yard field goal to give the Broncos a 23-20 overtime win.

"It showed a lot about our character to play with the adversity we had and come back in overtime," coach Mike Shanahan said.[19]

Trivia Test

Do the Broncos have an all-time winning or losing record in games played on artificial turf?

a) winning

b) losing

c) tied

Top 5 Wins over the Patriots

The Belichick/Brady Patriots were the top dog of the NFL for almost 20 years, but one place where their bark was louder than their bite was Denver, especially in the postseason. The Broncos have been involved in some terrific tussles with their East Coast rivals. Here are the top 5 Wins over the Patriots.

5. The First-Ever Broncos Game

The Broncos' rivalry with the Patriots goes back a long, long way. The then Boston Patriots hosted Denver in the first-ever regular season game in the history of the AFL. On September 9, 1960, Denver became the first team to win in the fledgling league, coming out on top 13-10 in front of a curious crowd of 21,597 at Boston University.

Al Carmichael wrote his name into the record books, catching a 59-yard pass from Frank Tripucka to become the team's (and league's) first touchdown scorer. The versatile Gene Mingo added another score courtesy of a 76-yard punt return.

Sporting a white and brown uniform combo, the Broncos had a very different look in their early years, one that was briefly resurrected in a throwback-inspired game in 2018.

Few watching this low-key opening game would have expected these two teams to become among the most dominant powers in professional sport over the next half century.

4. 1986 Divisional Round – Safety Seals It

Everyone remembers the 1986 AFC Championship Game against the Browns thanks to "The Drive" (see Top 5 Playoff Moments (Offense) for more), but not so many remember the game that got the Broncos there.

Dan Reeves' men welcomed New England for the Divisional Round playoff, the first time the old AFL rivals had met in a postseason game.

As is often the case in games involving these two old foes, there was little to choose between them. Rich Karlis gave the Broncos a 13-10 lead early in the second half, but a 45-yard Stanley Morgan touchdown on a flea flicker from Tony Eason put New England in the driver's seat. The Broncos responded with a 48-yard John Elway to Vance Johnson touchdown to take a 20-17 advantage.

Neither offense could get much going in the fourth quarter, but the Patriots had one last shot at tying the game. That potential shot was snuffed out by Rulon Jones on New England's final drive. The lineman sacked Eason for a safety to seal a 22-17 victory and send Denver to a conference decider in Cleveland.

3. 2005 Divisional Round – Champ's Pick

The Patriots arrived in Denver for the 2005 AFC Divisional Round playoff on the back of two Super Bowl wins and a 10-game unbeaten postseason run. It was a big task then for Jake Plummer and Co., but one they were more than up for.

An Adam Vinatieri field goal gave the Patriots a first-quarter lead, but that was about as good as it got for the visitors, who crumbled in the face of a dominant Denver defense.

Led by Champ Bailey, who intercepted two passes (returning one for 100 yards), the Broncos created five turnovers. Even punter Todd Sauerbrun got in on the act, forcing a fumble that led to a Jason Elam field goal.

The Broncos eventually ran out 27-13 winners to deliver a first playoff win at Invesco Field at Mile High and the first postseason victory since the Super Bowl XXXIII triumph over Atlanta.

The playoff push faltered against the Steelers a week later, but the win over the Patriots delivered some classic Mile High Magic.

2. 2015 Regular Season Appetizer

The 2015 Broncos showed they were made of the right stuff in a classic Sunday Night Football contest in Week 12. Missing the injured Peyton Manning, the Broncos were in trouble early with the unbeaten Patriots jumping out to a 14-0 lead early in the second quarter. Ronnie Hillman reduced the deficit, but the visitors regained their 14-point advantage in the fourth quarter thanks to a 63-yard Brandon Bolden touchdown.

With a blizzard blowing through Mile High, backup quarterback Brock Osweiler delivered arguably his best performance as a Bronco. Denver scored 17 unanswered points courtesy of a C. J. Anderson touchdown run, a Brandon McManus field goal, and a four-yard Osweiler to Caldwell TD connection with just 69 seconds on the clock. You get no gimmes from Tom Brady, though, who got the visitors into field goal range. Stephen Gostkowski duly obliged to send the game to overtime.

Denver lost the coin toss, but the defense restricted the Patriots to a three-and-out with the Broncos taking possession at their own 43. After a short run and quick completion to Owen Daniels, the Broncos inched into New England territory. Facing a crucial third-and-one, C. J. Anderson delivered one of the most memorable plays of the Super Bowl-winning season. Sweeping left with a convoy of blockers in front, #22 cantered his way into the snow-covered end zone for the game-winning score.

The win proved crucial, giving the Broncos the tiebreaker and home-field advantage in the playoffs. Which brings us to...

1. 2015 AFC Championship Game

After seeing off the Steelers 23-16 in the Divisional Round playoff, the Broncos set up a rematch with Bill Belichick and the Patriots. Just like the regular season clash, the AFC Championship Game was a tight, tense encounter.

This time, with Peyton Manning back at quarterback, it was the Broncos who jumped out to the early lead. A pair of Owen Daniels touchdowns and a McManus field goal gave the home side a 17-9 advantage at the half.

The teams exchanged field goals to set up an anxious final ten minutes. Twice the Patriots drove deep into Denver territory, and twice the stubborn Broncos defense held firm on fourth down.

Brady then showed just why he's one of the greatest ever. Facing a crucial fourth-and-10, he converted a 40-yard pass to Rob Gronkowski, then found his tight end on another fourth down, this time with just 12 seconds on the clock, for a touchdown that reduced the deficit to just two.

The New England comeback fell at the final hurdle courtesy of a great play from Aqib Talib, who tipped the game-tying pass into the hands of Bradley Roby for the pick, the win, and another AFC title.

Trivia Test

Who is the only Broncos back to rush for more than 200 yards in a game against the Patriots?

a) Terrell Davis

b) Knowshon Moreno

c) Clinton Portis

Drafts, Trades, Coaches, and GMs

Top 5 Undrafted Free Agents

The Broncos front office has a very happy knack of unearthing top talent from unorthodox places. At least one undrafted free agent made the starting 53-man roster in 18 of the past 19 seasons up to and including 2022. These players aren't there just to make up the numbers either. A select few have gone on to attain legendary status among Broncos Country. Here's our pick of the Top 5 Undrafted Free Agents.

5. Wesley Woodyard

Linebacker isn't the sexy position it was in the 1970s and 1980s. It's a dirty job stuffing the run and covering tight ends. There have been few better purveyors of this blue-collar skillset for the Broncos than Wesley Woodyard.

Overlooked by all 32 teams in the 2008 NFL Draft, the University of Kentucky star became a mainstay of the Broncos defense and special teams for six seasons. Woodyard more than deserved his elevation to full-time starter in 2012, registering three picks, 5.5 sacks, and 117 tackles.

After leaving Denver in 2014, Woodyard went on to enjoy a successful six-year stint with the Tennessee Titans.

Arguably the most impactful moment in Woodyard's life came off the field when he rescued a father and son who'd been involved in an auto accident in February 2021.

"Today I was driving on HW US 27 when a car driving the opposite direction of me flipped over. My hero mode kicked in. Next thing I know I'm pulling the dad out and crawling through the car to pull his son out of the car seat. Man that was scary."[20]

He might not have had the flash of other linebackers, but Woodyard's hard-grinding style made him a popular figure among Broncos Country.

4. C. J. Anderson

C. J. Anderson's place in Broncos' lore is assured courtesy of the two-yard touchdown run that put the icing on the team's Super Bowl 50 triumph over Carolina. Anderson was much more than just a one-hit wonder, though.

After signing with the Broncos in 2013, the five-foot-eight back's barreling style turned him into a firm favorite with the Mile High crowd. A key component of the 2015 Super Bowl-winning team, the former Cal back famously rumbled home for a 48-yard score to give the Broncos a crucial Week 12 overtime win over the Patriots.

That good form continued during a postseason that included 234 rushing yards, nine catches, two touchdowns, and, ultimately, a Super Bowl ring. After an injury-ravaged 2016, Anderson broke the 1,000-yard barrier for the first time in his career in 2017.

The former California Golden Bear bounced around the league following his departure from Denver, but he was in the right place at the right time when the Rams came calling in 2018, rushing for 299 yards in just two games to take the Rams to the postseason.

Now a running backs coach for Rice, Anderson's 3,051 rushing yards are still good for a place in the Top 10 on the Broncos' all-time rushing list.

3. Steve Watson

Undrafted free agent Steve Watson's career in orange started slowly. The former Temple wideout caught just 12 passes in his first two seasons as a pro. Not numbers that would indicate a legendary Bronco in the making. He exploded to life in 1981, though, becoming both a reliable pass catcher and a seriously dangerous deep threat. His 60 receptions that year went for 1,244 yards, an average of 20.7 yards per catch. Throw 13 touchdowns into the mix and it's easy to see why Pro Bowl and All-Pro recognition followed. His 95-yard touchdown reception against Detroit that year remains the longest by a Bronco since the 1970 merger.

Watson added two more 1,000-yard seasons to his impressive resume and became one of John Elway's favorite targets. By the time he hung up his cleats in 1987 he'd amassed 6,112 receiving yards and 36 touchdowns. Those figures put him in sixth place in franchise history. Perhaps most impressive was that following his rookie season, Watson's average never once dipped below 15 yards per catch.

Not bad for a kid who had been told by receivers coach Fran Polsfoot after the East-West Shrine Game, "You were so bad you couldn't catch a cold."[21]

2. Chris Harris Jr.

"Like a lot of guys who were snubbed in the draft, I play with a chip on my shoulder," wrote Chris Harris Jr. in his enlightening column on The Players' Tribune. "Every play is an opportunity to prove wrong everyone who did not recognize my talent."[22] And boy did he prove the doubters wrong...

In nine seasons in Denver, Harris Jr. started 121 games, picked off 20 passes, registered 4.5 sacks, racked up more than 500 tackles, and scored four touchdowns. Throw in four Pro Bowls, three All-Pro selections, and of course a Super Bowl ring and you have a truly sensational career.

The pinnacle of that superb career was undoubtedly the 2015 Super Bowl season when Harris was a key ingredient in an all-time great defense. A prime example being a crucial fourth-quarter pick-six in a Week 5 clash against the Raiders. Deep in Denver territory and requiring a field goal to take the lead, Harris picked off a Derek Carr pass and returned it for a 74-yard touchdown to give the Broncos a crucial 16-7 win.

To give an idea of just how dominant Harris was, consider that he didn't give up a single coverage touchdown from 2013 to 2015!

Aqib Talib might have had the swag and T. J. Ward the muscle, but the reassuring presence of Harris was the beating heart of the Broncos' "No Fly Zone."

1. Rod Smith

There's been no better undrafted free agent pickup in the history of the Broncos than Rod Smith. After a season on the practice squad, the Mississippi Southern alum gave a glimpse of what fans could expect in his NFL debut against Washington in 1995, catching a game-winning 43-yard touchdown with his first career catch to give the Broncos a 38-31 win.

There was plenty more of that to come, including 849 catches, 11,389 yards, and 68 touchdowns. And that's just the regular season. Another 49 catches for 860 yards and six touchdowns followed in playoff games.

The most iconic image of Smith for Broncos fans is probably his 80-yard touchdown catch in Super Bowl XXXIII against Atlanta. In other years his five catches for 152 yards and a score would have been good enough for MVP honors.

Of undrafted players only Antonio Gates has more receiving yards and Wes Welker more catches than Smith. That's pretty exalted company to be keeping.

The Broncos are seriously underrepresented in the Pro Football Hall of Fame. And there are few bigger omissions than Rod Smith.

Trivia Test

Which Bronco was the first undrafted rookie in NFL history to be invited to the Pro Bowl?

a) C. J. Anderson

b) Chris Harris Jr.

c) Philip Lindsay

Top 5 Terrific Trades

If you have a team that's ready to challenge, adding an extra piece via a timely trade can be just the thing to get you over the top. Get it wrong, though, and the wasted draft, salary, and personnel capital can set a team back years. The Broncos haven't been shy about pulling the trigger on a deal. Here are the Top 5 Terrific Trades.

5. Tony Jones

As contemporary Broncos fans know all too well, it's very difficult to run a competent offense if the big boys up front aren't up to the job. Denver bolstered its already handy o-line in 1997 by trading a second-round draft pick to Baltimore to acquire the services of Tony Jones.

Extremely tough but also versatile, the former Raven started at right tackle during the 1997 Super Bowl season before shifting to left tackle a year later en route to a second Super Bowl title.

Regardless of where he lined up, the scrappy Jones was a dominant presence on a truly great line. Jones spent the final four seasons of his 13-year career in Denver, starting 60 games. He earned his only Pro Bowl nod in 1998 as well as Second Team All-Pro honors.

Tragically, Jones died in January 2021 at the age of just 54.

4. Haven Moses

Speedy and reliable, the Broncos got a gem of a player when they sent defensive back Dwight Harrison to Buffalo in exchange for receiver Haven Moses (see Top 5 Shocking Moments for the backstory to this unorthodox trade). The former first-round pick enjoyed a superb career in Denver, catching 302 passes for 5,450 yards and 44 touchdowns during a 10-year spell with the Broncos.

The most eye-popping stat is the 18.0 yards per catch average, which remains the best by a Broncos receiver with at least 100 receptions. For three straight seasons during the 1970s, that figure was higher than 19 yards per catch.

The most memorable game in the former San Diego State star's career was a dominant performance against the arch-rival Raiders in the 1977 AFC Championship decider. Moses caught five passes for 168 yards and two touchdowns (including a 74-yard score) as the Broncos squeaked home by a score of 20-17.

A crucial element in turning the Broncos into one of the NFL's most respected teams, Moses was elected to the Ring of Fame in 1988.

3. Gary Zimmerman

Boasting a talented but inexperienced offensive line, the Broncos needed an old head to lead the group. And to protect John Elway's blind side. They ended up with the best in the business when they sent 1994 first- and sixth-round picks plus a fourth-rounder in 1995 to Minnesota to get Gary Zimmerman. The price was high but worth every penny as Zim went on to anchor one of the best position groups in NFL history.

The Broncos became the league's most dominant rushing attack and Zimmerman played a big part in it. The former USFL star started 76 games for the Broncos, was voted to three Pro Bowls, was named a First-Team All-Pro, and won his only championship ring at Super Bowl XXXII.

Zimmerman certainly enjoyed his time in the Mile High City. Speaking to DenverBroncos.com in August 2022, the star tackle said, "Coming to Denver was the best thing that ever happened to me. It was like I was adopted. The Broncos were like a family, just a great organization. Pat Bowlen was a fantastic owner. In the few times we ever lost, it was like letting my dad down."[23]

Thankfully for Broncos fans, those losses were rare. Zimmerman was elected to the Ring of Fame in 2003 and joined John Elway in the Pro Football Hall of Fame in 2008.

2. Champ Bailey

Champ Bailey made the Pro Bowl in four of his first five seasons with Washington but for some reason, the front office in DC didn't want to extend the contract of their star cornerback. Sensing an opportunity, Mike Shanahan put together a trade package that would bring Bailey to Denver (plus a second-round pick) with star rusher Clinton Portis heading in the opposite direction.

The trade was a rare instance of both sides getting what they wanted. Portis would go on to rush for almost 7,000 yards in Washington and Denver got a dominant corner for the next decade.

In 10 seasons with the Broncos, Bailey played 135 games, intercepted 34 passes (including a league-leading 10 in 2006), forced five fumbles and scored three touchdowns. The stats are only part of the story though. Bailey would usually line up against the opposition's premier receiver and more often than not, shut him down.

The former Georgia Bulldog was elected to eight Pro Bowls while with the Broncos and named a First-Team All-Pro three times. He helped the Broncos to five AFC West titles as well as an appearance in Super Bowl XLVIII.

Bailey was inducted into the Pro Football Hall of Fame at the first attempt in 2019, the first Broncos defender to receive recognition from Canton.

1. John Elway

When it comes to the biggest steals in history, the Broncos trading for John Elway is up there with the Mona Lisa being pinched from the Louvre and the multimillion-dollar Boston Brink's robbery.

Consider that all the Broncos gave up to acquire the services of one of the greatest players the NFL has ever seen was a first-round pick, quarterback Mark Hermann, and offensive lineman Chris Hinton. Granted, Hinton would go on to enjoy a very successful pro career but even so, the Broncos were the big, big winners from this extremely one-sided trade.

Elway (and his father, Jack) had made it crystal clear that he had zero interest in playing in Baltimore under owner Bob Irsay and coach Frank Kush, both notorious figures in NFL annals. He'd play baseball for a year, if need be, instead. Despite that, the Colts pulled the trigger on the rocket-armed Stanford quarterback with the first overall pick of the 1983 NFL Draft.

Cue plenty of cloak-and-dagger negotiations between Irsay and Broncos owner Edgar Kaiser, who eventually thrashed out what turned out to be the "Deal of the Century," for the Broncos at least. With that one trade, two franchises were transformed. The Colts snuck out of Baltimore for Indianapolis at the end of the season, and the Broncos were on their way to becoming one of the most successful teams in the league.

Trivia Test

John Elway was drafted by which team in the second round of the 1981 Major League Baseball Draft?

a) Boston Red Sox

b) Chicago Cubs

c) New York Yankees

Top 5 Free Agent Signings (Offense)

The draft provides the basis for most top rosters, but astute free agent signings come a close second. The Broncos have enjoyed some great success in the free agent market, signing some blue-chip superstars as well as unearthing some overlooked gems. Here are the Top 5 Free Agent signings on the offensive side of the ball.

5. Jake Plummer

After John Elway bowed out in magnificent style following Super Bowl XXXIII, the Broncos handed the quarterback reins to young Brian Griese. A middling 27-24 win-loss starting record and a single playoff appearance made coach Mike Shanahan look elsewhere for the start of the 2003 season.

The man he chose was Arizona signal caller Jake Plummer. The former second-round pick wasn't an obvious candidate for starting quarterback success given his mediocre .365-win percentage with the Cardinals. Plummer silenced the doubters by leading the Broncos to the postseason in each of his first three seasons in Denver.

"The Snake" hit his peak with the Broncos in 2005, steering the team to a 13-3 record, their first playoff win since the Elway era, and a place in the AFC Championship Game.

The freewheeling Plummer was always going to be on a short leash after the Broncos used the 11th pick of the 2006 NFL Draft on quarterback Jay Cutler. Benched following a Week 12 loss to the Chiefs, Plummer's time in Denver was effectively up.

Inconsistent he might have been but when on his game, Plummer was exhilarating to watch and provided plenty of thrills for a fanbase starved of recent success.

4. Ed McCaffrey

When the Broncos signed Ed McCaffrey in 1995, he didn't immediately strike Broncos Country as being a future superstar. The six-foot-five receiver had averaged just 25 catches a year in his first four seasons in the league with the Giants and 49ers, after all.

Mike Shanahan had been McCaffrey's offensive coordinator in San Francisco and liked what he'd seen from the gangly receiver. The former third-round pick justified that faith, becoming the perfect receiving foil for speedy Rod Smith and a terrific blocker on the outside for Terrell Davis.

A mainstay on the two 1990s Super Bowl-winning teams, Eddie Mc broke the 1,000-yard barrier for the first time in 1998 and received his only Pro Bowl nod.

In his nine years in Denver, the Stanford grad caught 462 passes for 6,200 yards and 49 touchdowns (plus another 36 for 490 yards and two scores in the postseason).

Inducted into the Colorado Sports Hall of Fame in 2022, McCaffrey also had a spell as the head coach of the University of Northern Colorado Bears.

3. Emmanuel Sanders

Needing help at wide receiver after Eric Decker's departure to the New York Jets, the Broncos struck gold with the addition of Emmanuel Sanders. The former Pittsburgh Steeler gave Peyton Manning and the Broncos a genuine triple threat alongside established stars Demaryius Thomas and Wes Welker.

In his first season in Denver in 2014, Sanders caught 101 passes for 1,440 yards (almost double his previous best yardage total while in Pittsburgh) with nine touchdown receptions. Further 1,000-yard seasons followed in 2015 and 2016 as well as two Pro Bowl nods and, of course, a Super Bowl ring. In fact, Sanders was the top receiver at Super Bowl 50, catching six passes for 83 yards.

Injury limited Sanders in his final two seasons in Denver. There were still plenty of memorable moments, though, including a first career touchdown pass in a nationally televised game against the Cardinals.

Speedy and sure-handed, Sanders was everything you could wish for from a free agent receiver.

2. Louis Vazquez

If you've gone all in on an aging star quarterback, you really, really need to protect him. Unglamorous as the position may be, a top-notch guard is essential if you want to give your prize asset the best opportunity for success.

With the arrival of Peyton Manning, a solid running game, and a stacked receiving corps, the only part of the offense lacking a little star power was the line. Step forward, Louis Vasquez.

The former Charger became the lynchpin of the line that took the Broncos to Super Bowl glory. A superb run blocker, Vasquez was dominant in pass protection too, not allowing a sack in 19 straight games during the 2013 regular season and playoffs. First-Team All-Pro and Pro Bowl recognition followed.

Surprisingly, the former third-round pick's final game as a Bronco (and final game in the NFL) was the Super Bowl 50 triumph over the Panthers.

His spell in Denver might have been relatively brief, but Vasquez had a big impact on the 2015 Super Bowl-winning team.

1. Peyton Manning

Many of the categories in this book have numerous contenders for the number one position. When it comes to the best free agent acquisitions on offense, there's only one name at the top and it's not even close. Peyton Williams Manning.

After signing for the Broncos following his release from Indianapolis, #18 rewrote not just the franchise but the NFL record books too. The numbers are extraordinary.

During his four seasons in Denver, Manning threw 151 touchdown passes in regular season and postseason play. He led the 2013 offense to an NFL-record 606 points, threw 55 touchdown passes, and won the NFL MVP Award. To put those touchdown passes into perspective, that total of 55 is more than double the number that John Elway managed in his best season! Of course, all those gaudy numbers and records count for little if there's no Super Bowl ring at the end.

Even though his physical powers were very much on the wane by 2015, Manning still had enough smarts and moxie to get the Broncos over the line when it really mattered. Most notably in the season finale against the Chargers. With a first or sixth seed position in the playoffs riding on the result, the stuttering Broncos were trailing midway through the third quarter with Brock Osweiler at QB. Needing a spark, Coach Kubiak called on his creaking leader. It wasn't particularly pretty but Manning steered the Broncos to a come-from-behind 27-20 win and home-field advantage throughout the postseason. The rest, as they say, is history.

Manning hung up his cleats after Super Bowl 50, becoming the first starting quarterback to win a Super Bowl title with two different teams.

A first-ballot Hall of Famer, Manning is undoubtedly an all-time Broncos great.

Trivia Test

Peyton Manning threw more regular season touchdown passes to which receiver than any other during his time with the Broncos?

a) Eric Decker

b) Demaryius Thomas

c) Julius Thomas

Top 5 Free Agent Signings (Defense)

Would the Broncos be a three-time Super Bowl champion without free agency? Probably not, especially when you look at the free agents that had such a huge impact on the defensive side of the ball on the Super Bowl-winning teams. Elite pass rushers and ball-hawking defensive backs dominate our list of the Top 5 Defensive Free Agent Signings.

5. T. J. Ward

After being manhandled by the Seahawks at Super Bowl XLVIII, the Broncos needed a change of direction. The move toward a brawnier defense began with the signing of Cleveland safety and noted thumper T. J. Ward.

The stat sheet for Ward's time in Denver doesn't really stand out. In three seasons with the Broncos, the former Cleveland Brown intercepted just three passes. Numbers, of course, only tell part of the story. Ward's leadership and tough tackling style were a perfect fit for an improving defense that really hit its straps in 2015. For any opposition receiver daring to venture into the middle of the field it became a potentially dangerous proposition.

Ward saved his best performance as a Bronco for the biggest stage of all, Super Bowl 50. Seven tackles, a fumble recovery, and an interception, the perfect end to a superb season.

The defensive back's spell in Denver wasn't a long one. Ward spent just one more season with the Broncos before heading south to Tampa Bay. His membership in the No Fly Zone on an all-time great team makes him one of the best free agent pickups in franchise history.

4. John Lynch

Tight in coverage, a hard hitter, and a nose for the ball. The ideal skillset for a successful NFL safety. And John Lynch was great at all three. The former Tampa Bay Buccaneer became a dominant presence on the Broncos defense in a four-season spell in Denver after signing as a free agent in 2004.

In those four seasons, Lynch registered 271 tackles, seven sacks, nine forced fumbles, and three interceptions.

The highlight of the Stanford graduate's Mile High run was 2005 when the stingy Broncos defense allowed just 16.1 points per game while building a 13-3 record and an appearance in the AFC Championship decider.

Alongside Champ Bailey and Aqib Talib, Lynch is one of just three Broncos to receive Pro Bowl recognition in each of his first four seasons in Denver.

Inducted into the Broncos Ring of Fame in 2016, Lynch became a member of the Pro Football Hall of Fame as part of the class of 2021.

3. Neil Smith

Cut by the Chiefs after a disappointing 1996 season, what better way for Neil Smith to stick it to the Kansas City brass than by signing with the hated Broncos?

The move was a gamble for both player and club, but it was one that paid rich rewards as Smith enjoyed a new lease of life on the Denver defensive line. During the 1997 Super Bowl run, the former second overall pick tied for the team lead alongside Alfred Williams and Maa Tanuvasa with 8.5 sacks.

Smith also delivered a crucial play in Super Bowl XXXII, recovering a fumble to set up a Jason Elam field goal.

The sack numbers weren't as high a year later, but Smith still had his moments during the Super Bowl defense. The pick of the highlight reel was a 79-yard fumble return touchdown in the Divisional Round playoff rout of Miami.

There aren't many NFL players that have a rule named after them, but Smith is one such example. The pass rusher was so adept at flinching to induce an offensive false start that authorities introduced the "Neil Smith Rule" to outlaw the maneuver.

2. Aqib Talib

There can't be many better free agent classes than the one John Elway put together in 2014. Joining Dallas pass rusher DeMarcus Ware and Cleveland safety T. J. Ward to add even more hustle to the backend was New England corner Aqib Talib. Throw Emmanuel Sanders into the mix and you have an all-time great crop.

Talib might not have been the most physically dominating defender, but when it came to swag and aggression, few could match the former Patriot.

The initial results under coordinator Jack Del Rio's reactive scheme were so-so, but when Wade Phillips returned to Denver as defensive coordinator in 2015, the Broncos found the perfect fit between scheme and personnel.

Talib was the personification of Phillips' ultra-aggressive, risk-taking style. Always playing right up to the edge (and sometimes over it), the former first-round pick never took a backward step. He picked off three passes during the Super Bowl season, returning two of them for touchdowns.

The fiery corner is the type of player you hate if he appears for the opposition, but you love to have on your side. We can't pay Talib a better compliment than that.

1. DeMarcus Ware

After a stellar career in Dallas that included a franchise-record 117 sacks, seven Pro Bowls, and four All-Pro nods, there was only one thing missing from DeMarcus Ware's footballing resume – a Super Bowl ring.

The former Cowboy remedied that during a dominant three-year spell in Denver. The stats weren't quite as splashy as those he notched up in Dallas, but whenever the Broncos needed a big play, you could usually rely on Ware to come up with the goods.

The 2015 Divisional Round playoff game is a case in point. With the Broncos trailing by a point in the fourth quarter and the Steelers in Denver territory and driving, Ware recovered a Fitzpatrick Toussaint fumble to give the home side a crucial turnover.

The perfect foil for Von Miller, Ware was a constant nuisance to Cam Newton in Super Bowl 50, registering 2.0 sacks and four quarterback pressures during the dominant Denver defense's world-class performance.

Ware delivered 25 sacks in 41 regular season and postseason starts for the Broncos as well as registering a pick and forcing four fumbles.

The consummate professional on and off the field, Ware was a perfect big-money free agent signing.

Trivia Test

Which of the following trio had the most sacks while with the Broncos?

a) Neil Smith

b) DeMarcus Ware

c) Alfred Williams

Top 5 Terrible Trades

Wheeling and dealing are crucial skills for a general manager. Finding value from players overlooked elsewhere can really boost a roster. The same goes for acquiring draft picks for players who might not have a future with the team. The Broncos have pulled off some real heists on the trading block. They've also been on the wrong end of some absolute shockers, including these 5 Terrible Trades.

5. Mike Pritchard

Wide receiver Mike Pritchard was a consistent performer in his first three seasons in the NFL. Picked 13th overall by Atlanta in the 1991 NFL Draft, the former Colorado Buffalo had 201 catches for 2,187 yards and 14 touchdowns in his time in Atlanta.

Solid but not spectacular numbers but enough to prompt Wade Phillips and the Denver front office to try and bring the receiver back to the Centennial State. The deal eventually agreed included the Broncos sending a 1994 third- and a 1995 first-round pick to the Falcons, who dealt Pritchard and a seventh to Denver.

Pritchard got off to a red-hot start in Denver, catching 19 passes for 271 yards in the first three games of the 1994 season. A freak lacerated kidney injury brought that highly promising season to a premature close in Week 4.

A year later, Pritchard managed just 33 catches for 441 yards and three touchdowns, and new coach Mike Shanahan decided to release him after the 1995 season.

The versatile receiver had his moments in Denver and might have gone on to enjoy a fine career had he stayed injury free. It's probably a bit harsh including Pritchard on this list, but 52 catches over two seasons don't represent great value for a player acquired after trading a first-round pick.

4. Joe Flacco

Joe Flacco broke Broncos fans' hearts after leading the Ravens to a brutal double-overtime playoff win in Denver in 2012.

There's no doubt that when the streaky Flacco was on, he was an extremely dangerous proposition. The problem was, you never quite knew when that would be. Ravens fans grew accustomed to lengthy spells of rather ordinary quarterback play in between the occasional burst of brilliance.

Still searching for the successor to Peyton Manning, the Broncos front office decided that the Super Bowl pedigree was worth a look and sent a fourth-round pick to Baltimore to acquire the 34-year-old. The Broncos also took on the remainder of the six-foot-six signal caller's three-year, $63 million contract.

There wasn't much gas left in the Flacco tank when he arrived in Denver, as witnessed by a six-touchdown, five-interception stat line in eight starts for the Broncos.

As Flacco's contract wasn't guaranteed, the Broncos cut short the experiment after just one disappointing season.

Beware of signing a player who has impressed against you. Which brings us to our next selection.

3. Matt Robinson

The defending AFC champion Broncos suffered one of the worst defeats in franchise history in Week 10 of the 1978 season. Despite leading 28-7 in the second quarter, the Broncos collapsed to a 31-28 defeat to the New York Jets, led by quarterback Matt Robinson, who had started the season as the backup. A 75-yard touchdown pass to Wesley Walker late in the fourth quarter sealed the deal for Gang Green.

On the lookout for a quarterback two years later, the Broncos remembered the name and sent 1980 first- and 1981 second-round picks as well as backup QB Craig Penrose to the Jets to acquire Robinson's services.

Robinson started seven games for the Broncos, and a 4-3 win-loss record looks decent enough. Sadly, just two touchdowns and 12 interceptions tell the story more clearly. The former Jet was cut, spending two seasons as a backup in Buffalo, then two more playing in the USFL.

2. Jay Cutler

Jay Cutler might not be everyone's cup of tea. The sometimes sullen body language wasn't great, for sure. Still, he'd shown steady improvement in his first three seasons in the League, culminating in a Pro Bowl nod in 2008 after a 4,500-yard, 25-touchdown season. Plenty for new head coach Josh McDaniels to work with you'd think? Or maybe not.

Cutler didn't play for the Broncos again after a spectacular falling out with a rookie head coach eager to stamp his authority on his new team.

The Broncos traded their flame-throwing quarterback plus a 2009 fifth-round pick to the Chicago Bears in exchange for quarterback Kyle Orton, first- and third-round picks in 2009, plus another first-round pick in 2010.

That's a big haul. But only if you use those picks wisely. With those extra selections the Broncos added solid defensive end Robert Ayers, cornerback bust Alphonso Smith, and tight end Richard Quinn, who didn't register a single catch in his NFL career. A pretty underwhelming bunch compared to a franchise quarterback.

Given different circumstances, Cutler's career might have panned out very differently.

1. Russell Wilson

As a Broncos fan, I'm hoping that this selection makes me look extremely silly. In a perfect world, you're reading this after the 2023 season and Russell Wilson has defied expectations and been named NFL Comeback Player of the Year after a stunning return to form.

Unfortunately, I'm writing this after the 2022 season. And what a disaster of a season it has been, filled with questionable coaching, historically bad offensive play, and potentially, one of the worst trades in NFL history.

The Broncos thought they'd solved their post-Manning quarterback woes courtesy of a blockbuster trade with the Seahawks to nab the services of Russell Wilson. The nine-time Pro Bowler didn't come cheaply. The Broncos sent quarterback Drew Lock, tight end Noah Fant, defensive lineman Shelby Harris, plus 2022 first, second-, and fifth round and 2023 first-and second-round picks to Seattle to get their man.

After the first season, it looks as if the Seahawks have got away with the biggest robbery in America since the Boston Gallery Heist. Wilson's performance was nothing short of disastrous during 2022. A 3-11 starting record, just 13 touchdowns and 10 interceptions represent scant reward after giving up a relative king's ransom. Even worse is the five-year contract extension, which includes $165 million in guarantees. Yikes.

Unless Sean Payton helps prompt a Lazarus-like comeback, the Russell Wilson trade will go down as one of the worst in NFL, let alone Broncos, history.

Trivia Test

Russell Wilson's first touchdown pass as a Bronco was a 67-yarder to which receiver?

a) Jerry Jeudy

b) Courtland Sutton

c) Javonte Williams

Top 5 Head Coaches

You don't become one of the NFL's most successful franchises without top-quality coaching. The Broncos have hired some blue-chip brains to orchestrate the on-field talent. Three Super Bowl titles and eight Super Bowl appearances require some high-class hires. Here are the Top 5 Head Coaches.

5. John Fox

After the chaos of the Josh McDaniels era, the Broncos needed a grown-up. Someone who'd been around the block a few times and knew his way around an NFL locker room. John Fox seemed to fit that bill. Fox might have had plenty of experience, but after being fired by Carolina after a 2-14 season, he wasn't quite the sexy pick many in Broncos Country hoped for. The hire turned out to be just what the Broncos needed, though.

The Fox era might not have delivered a Super Bowl title, but it provided some of the most memorable moments in franchise history. Riding the wave of Tebowmania, the Fox-led Broncos made it to the postseason in 2011. With the addition of Peyton Manning a year later, Denver produced some of the most spectacular offense in the history of the NFL. The only thing missing was a Super Bowl and the Broncos got close.

Fox's reign ended on quite a sour note following a hugely disappointing 2014 Divisional Round playoff loss to the Colts. With the Peyton Manning Super Bowl window closing, GM John Elway took the nuclear option and fired Fox. History has proved it was the right move.

Four division titles in four seasons combined with the best winning percentage of any coach in franchise history represent a pretty good return for John Fox, especially considering the mess he inherited from Josh McDaniels.

4. Red Miller

John Ralston left the Broncos in pretty good shape when he stepped down as head coach following a 9-5 1976 season. His replacement, Red Miller, built on those solid foundations to create one of the best teams in franchise history.

Under Miller's watch, the Broncos bagged a first AFC West title, a first postseason appearance, a first playoff win, and a first visit to the Super Bowl. That 1977 run earned Miller AP NFL Head Coach of the Year honors.

The Broncos never quite hit those heights again under Miller but became one of the league's most consistent and respected teams. Denver never endured a losing season in Miller's four-year stint as head coach, winning 40 games and losing just 22. He led the team to back-to-back division titles and three successive playoff berths and will always be associated with one of the NFL's all-time great defenses, the Orange Crush.

Fired following an 8-8 season in 1980, Miller was inducted into the Broncos Ring of Fame in 2017.

3. Dan Reeves

The first head coach to steer the Broncos to 100 wins and multiple Super Bowl appearances, there was plenty for fans to enjoy during Dan Reeves' tenure as head coach. In 12 seasons in Denver, the former Dallas tight end led the Broncos to the playoffs six times, won five AFC West titles, and made three Super Bowl appearances. Only twice did the Broncos register a losing record with Reeves at the helm.

The coach's relationship with quarterback John Elway wasn't always the smoothest (see the Top 5 Feuds and Fallouts for more on this), but the pair combined to deliver some fantastic action for Broncos Country. "The Drive" and "The Fumble" both came under Reeves' watch.

Axed by Pat Bowlen after a middling 8-8 season in 1992, Reeves later enjoyed moments of success with the Giants and Falcons. The Georgian was in charge of the Atlanta team that was beaten by the Broncos at Super Bowl XXXIII.

Despite the lack of a Super Bowl triumph, Reeves was a hugely influential figure in the history of the team and brought consistent success for more than a decade.

2. Gary Kubiak

"Getting the band back together" sounds great to nostalgic ears but doesn't often result in success. One rare exception was the return to Denver of longtime offensive coordinator Gary Kubiak. Hired by friend and former teammate John Elway to replace John Fox as head coach, Kubiak brought along Wade Phillips and Rick Dennison to add even more old-school Broncos flavor.

The retro-tinged coaching staff proved an inspired combination, taking the Broncos to a Super Bowl title in their first season together. In doing so, Kubiak became the first head coach to both play in and coach the same team in a Super Bowl.

The 2015 Kubiak/Manning offense might not have offered the spectacular pyrotechnics of previous seasons, but they got the job done whenever it was really needed. Kubes got the big decisions right too, bringing Manning from the bench to stir a crucial comeback in the season finale against San Diego.

Coach Kubiak lasted just one more season as a head coach, stepping down due to health concerns. His tenure in Denver might have been short, but with a precious Super Bowl ring in the bag, Kubiak goes down as our number two head coach.

1. Mike Shanahan

Combine a great head coach with a Hall of Fame quarterback and magic can happen. The Broncos were the beneficiaries of such alchemy when Mike Shanahan was reunited with John Elway in Denver in 1995.

Twice an assistant in Denver, Shanahan started slowly as a head coach with an 8-8 year. The three seasons that followed are among the best in the history of the NFL. In that stretch the Broncos won 39 regular season games and lost just nine, were unbeaten at home, and, oh yes, claimed the not so insignificant matter of back-to-back Super Bowl titles.

Even when talismanic quarterback John Elway retired, the Broncos were always competitive under Shanahan. The Broncos endured just two losing seasons in his 14 years as head coach and made the playoffs seven times in all.

There aren't many coaches who get a system named after them, but the hugely influential zone running scheme popularized by Mike and, later, son Kyle is rightly known as the Shanahan offense.

Shanahan's 138 regular season wins are the most in franchise history. So are his eight victories in the postseason. When it comes to legendary figures in the history of the Broncos, Mike Shanahan is right up there with the best of them.

Trivia Test

What was coach Red Miller's given first name?

a) Richard

b) Robert

c) Roderick

Top 5 Head Coach Calamities

To be named a head coach in the NFL, you're one of the best in the business. The trouble is, all the other 31 head coaches are among the best in the business too. Even if you're dedicated, hardworking, and super talented, you can still look like a chump if the cards don't fall kindly. Here are five head coaches whose reigns left a little to be desired.

5. Lou Saban

Hopes were high when Lou Saban rode into Denver in 1967. The former Browns linebacker arrived in the Mile High City with a coaching resume that included back-to-back AFL championships with the Bills in 1964 and 1965.

The Broncos gave their new man a 10-year contract, hoping that he could work the same magic that had turned Buffalo from also-rans to champions. Despite plenty of wheeling and dealing and his trademark, high-intensity coaching style, it never quite worked out for the former AFL Coach of the Year.

The Broncos won just 20 out of 65 games with Saban at the helm, never achieving a winning record. The head coach did the honorable thing and called time on his career in Denver after a disappointing 2-6-1 start to the 1971 season.

Saban returned to Buffalo in 1972, steering the Bills to a winning record in three of the following four years. He later enjoyed a lengthy career coaching in the college ranks, eventually hanging up his whistle in 2002 at the age of 80. Unusually for a football man, Saban also had a two-year stint as the president of the New York Yankees in the early 1980s.

4. Vic Fangio

After the experiment with novice Vance Joseph turned sour, the Broncos wanted a coach with plenty of NFL experience entering the 2019 season. And they didn't come much more NFL savvy than 60-year-old Vic Fangio, a man who might as well have been born in sweatpants with a whistle round his neck.

The hugely experienced Fangio had just crafted one of the NFL's elite defenses in Chicago, a unit that had led the league in scoring and turnovers and finished third in yards allowed.

As one of the most innovative defensive coaches of the modern era, the Broncos could expect a seriously stingy defense if nothing else. It took a while, but that defense did become one of the league's elite outfits by Fangio's third season in charge. Even then, the team could never seem to get a big stop or a turnover when required as Wade Phillips' squads had done.

With the perennial quarterback woes, the underwhelming offense couldn't score enough points and the Broncos ended up in the AFC West basement in two of Fangio's three seasons in charge.

Like defensive geniuses Dick LeBeau and our own Wade Phillips, Fangio seems best suited to being a superb coordinator rather than a head coach.

3. Vance Joseph

Combine an untried, defensive-minded head coach with an underwhelming quarterback room and the results aren't likely to be explosive. In a good way at least. That's just what the Broncos did when they hired Vance Joseph in early 2017 and tried to eke out a competent offense with Trevor Siemian, Brock Osweiler, Paxton Lynch, and later Case Keenum at the controls.

Add some questionable clock and game management into the mix and it wasn't really a recipe for success. The defense in the Joseph era wasn't bad. But it didn't dominate in a manner that could carry a team all the way to a playoff appearance either. And with an offense that ranked 27th and 24th in points scored, that defense needed to be really good.

In two seasons in Denver, the Broncos finished with 5-11 and 6-10 records. That left Joseph with the dubious honor of being the first head coach since the early 1970s to lead the team to back-to-back losing records.

2. Josh McDaniels

The Fangio and Joseph eras in Denver were both a bit meh. Sure, they were disappointing, but they weren't complete train wrecks that had the rest of the league gawping in astonishment. The final two names on our list managed just that, starting with Josh McDaniels.

There was never a dull moment in the former New England offensive guru's two-year stint in Denver, which included feuding with star players, trading a franchise quarterback, winning streaks followed by even longer barren runs, spy scandals, handshake scandals, and highly contentious draft picks.

Boring it most certainly wasn't. Neither was it successful. A coach can ride out all manner of controversies if they consistently add to the W column. The Broncos under McDaniels didn't manage that. After winning his first six games, McDaniels won only five of the 22 that followed, and he was canned with four games left of the 2010 season.

The McDaniels era was quite the ride for Broncos Country, but it's not a train we're keen on boarding again any time soon.

1. Nathaniel Hackett

Poor old Nathaniel Hackett. Charged in 2022 with lifting the Broncos from a slough of mediocrity and with a supposed franchise quarterback at his disposal, he served up one of the worst seasons in living memory.

It wasn't just the losses, it was the shambling manner of those losses. The Broncos often looked a beat behind where they should have been, in terms of play calling, clock management, and in-game decision making. Having the crowd counting down the play clock to avoid yet another delay of game penalty verges on the humiliating.

The offense under Hackett's tenure was almost unwatchable at times, record breaking in its awfulness. Injuries didn't help. Neither did Russell Wilson, whose form cratered from Hall of Famer to practice squad possible in the space of a few weeks. It all happened on Hackett's watch, though, and it was extremely difficult to comprehend.

The Hackett era was reminiscent of a classic episode of the TV comedy *Frasier* where the radio psychiatrist tries to get a new contract from his station, KACL. Instead of retaining his tough-as-nails agent Bebe for the negotiations, he opts instead for the genial, ethical agent and part-time boy scout leader Ben, with suitably disastrous results.

The former Green Bay assistant seems like a perfectly amiable and genuine chap. Like Frasier's agent, Hackett seemed way out of his depth in this particular role.

Trivia Test

Which of the following three head coaches had the best winning percentage while in charge of the Broncos?

a) Vic Fangio

b) Vance Joseph

c) Josh McDaniels

Top 5 Late Round Steals

First-round picks may get all the hype in the NFL Draft, but there are uncut gems ready for polishing lower down the order. The Broncos have found some serious talent in the nether reaches of the draft. Here are our Top 5 Late Round Steals.

5. Tyrone Braxton

Tyrone Braxton was always a grafter. Summer jobs included grave digger and riding a garbage truck. The North Dakota State defensive back's life was transformed when the Broncos selected him with the penultimate pick of the 1987 NFL Draft (334th out of 335 players selected).

From those inauspicious beginnings, Braxton went on to enjoy a superb career in Denver, winning two Super Bowls and appearing in two more. In his 12 seasons in the Mile High City, Braxton played in 182 regular season and playoff games, registering 37 interceptions, forcing eight fumbles, and scoring four touchdowns. He led the NFL in picks in 1996 with nine and received his only Pro Bowl nod.

Braxton sealed his place in Broncos folklore by intercepting a Brett Favre pass in Super Bowl XXXII to set up a Denver touchdown.

Speaking to DenverBroncos.com, coach Mike Shanahan said, "On paper, Tyrone looked too short, too slow and too small but we play the games on the field, and he was always an outstanding player and had a great feel for the game."[24]

Not bad for a 12th-round pick.

4. Tom Nalen

When the Broncos traded wide receiver Arthur Marshall to the Giants for a late pick in the last round of the 1994 NFL Draft, they couldn't have expected to find a franchise player. But that was exactly what they got in the form of Boston College offensive lineman Tom Nalen.

The seventh-round center became the lynchpin of one of the best offensive lines in NFL history. In a 14-year career, Nalen was voted to the Pro Bowl five times and was twice named a First Team All-Pro. He was also the NFL's Offensive Lineman of the Year for 2003. Add a pair of Super Bowl rings and you have a marvelous career.

An incredible 11 different rushers enjoyed 1,000-yard seasons pounding the rock behind lines led by Nalen. Terrell Davis, Clinton Portis, and Mike Anderson don't get their record-breaking seasons without Nalen and company leading the way.

Considering just how physically demanding it can be to play on the offensive line, Nalen's durability was incredible. Only John Elway has more starts for the Broncos than Nalen's 188.

We'll leave the last word to #7, who described his offensive colleague as "the epitome of grit, toughness & athleticism."[25]

3. Karl Mecklenburg

John Elway wasn't the only legend to join the Broncos in 1983. The Broncos took a punt on a raw but talented defender in the 12th and final round that year (310th overall). That pick was Karl Mecklenburg and it turned into paydirt as the former Minnesota Golden Gopher became a core component of the Denver defense for the next decade.

Mecklenburg began his pro career as a defensive end but really found his groove after moving to linebacker. In 12 seasons in Denver, he started 141 games, registered more than 1,100 tackles, forced 16 fumbles, and picked off five passes. At the time of his retirement in 1994, Mecklenburg's 79 sacks were the most in franchise history. He is the only Bronco to register four sacks in a game more than once.

Voted to the Pro Bowl six times and named a First-Team All-Pro on three occasions, Mecklenburg was added to the Broncos Ring of Fame in 2001.

"I was a 12th-round draft choice; nobody expected me to make it, because height, weight, 40 time, I didn't match up," Mecklenburg told DenverBroncos.com. "But I found out early on in my career if you could take the first step in the right direction before anybody else did, all the angles would change in your favor. The tight end couldn't pin you in, the guard couldn't cut you off, the fullback couldn't keep you from getting to the line of scrimmage – everything changed. And that was really my career."[26]

And what a career it was.

2. Shannon Sharpe

Coming out of Savannah State, Shannon Sharpe was considered a classic "tweener." Not quite big enough to play tight end but not quite quick enough to be an elite NFL receiver. That can be the only explanation as to why Sharpe dropped all the way to the seventh round of the 1990 NFL Draft.

Selected by the Broncos with the 192nd overall pick, Sharpe's career in orange started slowly. After catching just 29 passes in his first two seasons, the chirpy tight end enjoyed a breakout season in 1992, earning the first of six straight Pro Bowl nods.

In two spells in Denver, Sharpe caught 675 passes, second only to the great Rod Smith in franchise history. His 8,439 receiving yards and 55 touchdowns are good for third in the team record books. In a 2002 overtime win at Kansas City, #84 became the first Bronco to enjoy a 200-yard receiving game.

A crucial member of the 1997 and 1998 Super Bowl championship teams, Sharpe added a third Super Bowl to his bulging resume during a brief spell in Baltimore. A member of the 1990s NFL All-Decade Team, he was inducted into the Pro Football Hall of Fame in 2011.

Looking back on his spectacular career in 2021, Sharpe said, "You can measure how fast I am, how high I can jump. You can't measure my passion. My desire to beat the man across from me. I got three Super Bowl wins, I got eight Pro Bowls under my belt and a gold jacket. I won."[27]

And so did the Broncos.

1. Terrell Davis

Fifteen running backs were selected in the 1995 NFL Draft before the Broncos took a flier on an oft-injured Georgia Bulldog with the 197th pick. That sixth-round pick turned out to be one of the biggest steals in the history of the National Football League.

Terrell Davis would go on to become *the* dominant offensive player of the late 1990s, smashing a host of records in the process.

In his first four seasons as a pro, Davis rushed for a mind-boggling 6,413 yards. In 1998, he became just the fourth rusher to break the 2,000-yard barrier while being named the league MVP. Oh, and we almost forgot to mention that he scored 23 touchdowns during that record-breaking season.

If the regular season stats are amazing, the postseason numbers are even more extraordinary. I've written about TD's playoff performances in a previous chapter but they're so incredible they bear repeating.

Davis rushed for 100 yards or more in seven straight postseason games. He totaled 1,140 rushing yards from just 204 carries at an average of 5.6 yards per carry in eight playoff appearances. Add 12 postseason touchdowns, two rings, and a Super Bowl MVP Award and you have an all-time great career.

Davis was never the same after suffering a knee injury while making a tackle following an interception in a 1999 game against the Jets. For that golden four-year period prior, there was arguably no more dominant back in the history of the game.

Finally recognized by the voting panel in Canton, Davis was eventually inducted into the Pro Football Hall of Fame in 2017.

Trivia Test

Terrell Davis first gained notice following a fantastic special teams hit in a preseason game against the 49ers. In what city did that game take place?

a) London

b) Munich

c) Tokyo

Top 5 Draft Busts

Draft and develop is a key element of NFL success. Get it right with a crop of good, young talent (and their cheap salaries) and you'll be set for seasons to come. Get it wrong and it can put a team on the back foot for years. Of course, player evaluation is far from an exact science. Here are five examples of what looked like premium talent but turned out to be fool's gold.

5. Alphonso Smith

To whiff on a high-value draft pick is always disappointing. Even more so if you trade up to get him. The Broncos did just that with cornerback Alphonso Smith, agreeing to a deal with Seattle to move up to the 37th pick to select the Wake Forest DB.

Trading up early in the second round deserves some decent compensation, but a future first-round pick? That was what the Broncos gave up to acquire Smith. That 2010 draft choice turned into the 14th overall pick, a pick the Seahawks used to select safety Earl Thomas. No arguing about who got the better of that deal.

If Smith had turned out to be a star, the extremely high compensation might have been worth it. Alas for Broncos Country, Smith was a colossal bust. Unable to crack the starting lineup, his Broncos career consisted of just 15 games, 14 tackles, and no interceptions.

The front office cut their losses after a single season, trading Smith to Detroit for seventh-round tight end Dan Gronkowski.

4. Marcus Nash

Fresh from a first Super Bowl triumph, the Broncos were on the hunt for a receiver to complement Rod Smith, Ed McCaffrey, and Shannon Sharpe. They thought they'd found the answer in Marcus Nash. The speedy wideout had dazzled alongside Peyton Manning at Tennessee and the Broncos used the 30th overall pick to get their man.

Sadly, Nash caught just four passes as a Bronco before being traded to Miami two games into the 1999 season for another draft bust, John Avery. A fresh start didn't help either player with neither making a lasting impression in their new locale.

Baltimore had a brief look at Nash but quickly moved on. That might have been the end for the former college star, but perseverance eventually paid. After trying out with Winnipeg in the CFL, he caught on in the Arena League, becoming a star performer for the Las Vegas Gladiators and Dallas Desperadoes.

After six seasons of Arena Football, a neck injury brought Nash's pro career to an abrupt and premature end in 2008.

3. Paxton Lynch

The Broncos' attempt to draft a franchise quarterback goes on and on and on. In 2016, they used the 26th overall pick to select Paxton Lynch. Surprisingly mobile for a six-foot-seven, 240-pound quarterback, and with an arm that could really zing it, Lynch had all the attributes of a prototype NFL signal caller.

The third quarterback taken behind Jared Goff and Carson Wentz, Lynch was a disappointment right from the get-go. Unable to wrestle the starting job from seventh-round pick Trevor Siemian, Lynch seemingly worked his way down rather than up the depth chart.

In total, Lynch started just four games for the Broncos, throwing four touchdowns and four picks while amassing a 1-3 starting record.

With question marks about his hunger and work ethic, Lynch couldn't budge Case Keenum or even Chad Kelly. The team cut him just before the start of the 2018 season after claiming Kevin Hogan (who?) off waivers. An ignominious end for a terrible pick.

Lynch bounced around to Seattle and then Pittsburgh before grabbing a third-string gig with the Saskatchewan Roughriders in the Canadian Football League. You have to admire Lynch's perseverance. The quarterback made his debut with the XFL's Orlando Guardians in February 2023.

2. Jarvis Moss

After a great performance for Florida in the National Championship Game against Ohio State, defensive lineman Jarvis Moss was a hot property heading into the 2007 NFL Draft. Mike Shanahan and the Broncos front office had their heads turned by the dominant defender, sending third- and fifth-round picks to the Jags to jump up from 21st to 17th to get their man.

The all-action, All-American college defender was nowhere to be seen when he made the transition to the pros. He stuck around with the team, playing 34 games for Denver, but never dazzled. A total of 24 tackles, 3.5 sacks, and a forced fumble represent slim returns from a three-and-a-half-season stint with the Broncos.

Josh McDaniels tried to light a fire under Moss by moving him from defensive end to linebacker but that didn't pan out either.

The play Moss is probably best known for is a holding penalty that negated a spectacular kickoff return touchdown in the Broncos' loss to the 49ers in London in 2012.

After his release by the Broncos, Moss wound up with division rival Oakland. They couldn't work out the Moss magic formula either and the big defensive lineman was out of football by 2011.

1. Ted Gregory

These days, teams know virtually everything there is to know about potential draft picks, down to the last toenail. Even with all that knowledge, picking a dud is very much an occupational hazard. Things were a bit more slapdash when it came to research in the 1980s and there's no greater example than the selection of Ted Gregory.

Hoping for a gritty addition to the defensive line, the Broncos used the 26th pick in the 1988 NFL Draft on the Syracuse tackle. When their prize new signing arrived in Denver he weighed in at a distinctly un-tackle-like 260 pounds, and at five-foot-nine was much shorter than the listed six-foot-one. Add persistent knee trouble into the mix and it didn't take long for the Broncos to realize they'd dropped a massive bollock.

They moved swiftly, sending Gregory to New Orleans in a swap deal for fellow defensive lineman and first-round bust Shawn Knight. The knee issues manifested themselves quickly and Gregory's NFL career amounted to just three games. His only sack as a pro came in a 42-0 New Orleans rout, ironically against the Broncos in Week 12.

Trivia Test

Paxton Lynch played college ball at which southern school?

a) Auburn

b) Memphis

c) Tennessee

Top 5 Free Agent Flops

Not every free agent class can match the one the Broncos put together in 2014. Then again, it would be pretty difficult to land a quartet as accomplished as T. J. Ward, DeMarcus Ware, Aqib Talib, and Emmanuel Sanders. Signing just one player of that caliber a season isn't bad going. Sadly, for Broncos Country, the front office has had buyer's remorse with a few of their big-ticket items. Here are the Top 5 Free Agent Flops.

5. Case Keenum – The Journeyman's Journeyman

Case Keenum can consider himself a little unlucky to make this list. Compared to some of the chancers who have stolen a living from the Broncos, Keenum was a consummate professional – dedicated, hardworking, and thoroughly committed to the cause. He just wasn't quite good enough.

The Broncos quarterback situation has been a dumpster fire since Peyton Manning rode off into the sunset. After trying to get a spark from Trevor Siemian, Brock Osweiler, and Paxton Lynch, GM John Elway turned to Keenum, fresh off a career year in Minnesota.

After guiding the 2017 Vikings to a surprise NFC Championship Game appearance, Keenum hit the free agency jackpot in Denver, inking a two-year, $36 million deal with $25 million guaranteed.

Alas for Broncos Country, Keenum turned out to be more Kyle Orton than John Elway. Not a total disaster but nowhere near good enough for a team with postseason aspirations. Despite throwing for a career-high 3,890 yards with the Broncos, the front office exchanged late-round picks with Washington and called time on the Keenum era after a single 6-10 season.

Keenum is one of the best backup quarterbacks in the NFL. Solid and steady, he won't gift too many games to the opposition. He just won't win too many on his own either.

4. Daryl Gardener

In six seasons in Miami and another in Washington, Daryl Gardener had developed into a sturdy NFL defensive lineman. Just the attributes the Broncos were looking for when they were in the market for a veteran run stuffer heading into the 2003 season.

Such talents don't come cheap. Gardener signed a seven-year deal worth almost $35 million including a $5 million signing bonus. For that hefty investment, the Broncos got a grand total of three starts from the former first-round draft pick.

Gardener's stay in Denver was disastrous from the outset. A brawl outside a pancake house (!) resulted in not only an arrest but also a wrist injury that kept him out of training camp. That injury meant he also missed the first four games of the season.

The tackle was later suspended not once but twice for "conduct detrimental to the team." A sure-fire way to get into the doghouse is to publicly disrespect the head coach. Gardener did that too, describing Mike Shanahan as "that little man up there" during a radio interview. All told, Gardener played five games in Broncos colors.

The Broncos reached a settlement with Gardener, allowing them to cut their losses on this disastrous signing. Gardener never played in the NFL again but later tried his luck on the bodybuilding circuit.

3. Dale Carter – Cornerback Calamity

The Broncos knew all about Dale Carter. The cornerback had been a cornerstone of the Kansas City secondary for seven years, earning a host of honors including NFL Defensive Rookie of the Year and four straight Pro Bowl selections from 1994 to 1997.

When the Broncos pulled the trigger on signing Carter, they thought they were getting a blue-chip talent who would shore up the defensive backfield for years to come. Carter on one side and Champ Bailey on the other – what's not to like? Well, quite a lot actually.

Carter's time in Denver proved to be highly controversial. The defensive back was caught on camera aiming a loogie at Jacksonville tackle Tony Boselli and later ran foul of NFL drug testers. A repeat offender, Carter was subsequently banned for the whole of the 2000 season.

The off-field shenanigans might have been forgiven if the results on the field had been spectacular. They weren't. Carter had just two interceptions in 14 games as the Broncos crashed to a hugely disappointing 6-10 season.

After serving his 12-month suspension Carter had spells with Minnesota, New Orleans, and Baltimore. The aberration in Denver is best forgotten by all concerned.

2. Menelik Watson – Missing Mancunian Muscle

Since first hitting national TV screens in the 1980s, the NFL has exploded in popularity in the UK. Bar the odd kicker, us Brits are still waiting for our first homegrown hero to become a huge NFL star. We had high hopes for Menelik Watson.

The Manchester-born offensive lineman's route to the NFL was highly unusual. A schoolboy soccer player, Watson turned to basketball, was spotted by an American scout, and ended up with a scholarship at Marist College in New Jersey. That didn't quite work out and after giving boxing a try, the six-foot-six Watson ended up on the football field at Saddleback Community College in California. Despite knowing nothing about the game, the o-lineman was a quick learner and gained a roster spot at Florida State.

The rapid ascent continued, with the transition from complete novice to the NFL taking just two years. Physically gifted but technically raw, the Raiders took a punt on Watson in the second round of the 2013 NFL Draft. After four injury-ravaged seasons in Oakland, Watson signed a three-year, $18 million contract with the Broncos in 2017.

Unhappily, for Broncos Country and British fans, Watson wasn't the answer to Denver's perennial problems at right tackle. Hit once again by the injury bug, the Mancunian played just seven games for the Broncos and was released after one season.

The Watson story is an amazing one. A shame then that it doesn't come with a happier ending.

1. Ja'Wuan James – 63 Snaps

After the Menelik Watson experiment ended in failure, the Broncos were once again looking for an upgrade at the tackle position. John Elway broke the bank, offering a $51 million contract (with $27 million guaranteed) to the talented but oft-injured Ja'Wuan James.

Drafted 19th overall by the Dolphins in 2014, James played 62 out of a possible 80 games during a five-season stint in Miami. This was a high-risk but potentially high-reward play from the Broncos front office and one that proved to be a big whiff.

A knee injury restricted James to just 63 snaps in three games throughout the whole of the 2019 season. That was 63 more than 2020 when James sat out the year because of Covid. Hoping for a fresh start on all sides, the Broncos had inked the former Tennessee Volunteer as their right tackle for the 2021 season. An off-season Achilles tear put paid to that as James missed the entire year.

As the injury took place away from the team's practice facility, the Broncos baulked at paying a $15 million guaranteed portion of his salary. The team and player eventually agreed to a $1.09 million settlement.

The disastrous James signing is one that the Broncos would really like to do over.

Trivia Test

Fumble-prone running back Melvin Gordon joined the Broncos as a free agent after five seasons with which team?

a) Chargers

b) Chiefs

c) Raiders

The Fun Stuff (With a Couple of Serious Categories Thrown In)

Top 5 Comebacks

Victories from seemingly unwinnable positions, the return of an old friend, a physical resurgence following a very serious injury, and an amazing individual performance take top billing in the Top 5 Comebacks in franchise history.

5. Drew Lock's Dream Game

There weren't too many highlights to cheer during the Drew Lock era in Denver. Occasional flashes of brilliance, sure. Sustained excellence, not so much. One exception was an amazing comeback win over the Chargers in November 2020.

Trailing 24-3 midway through the third quarter, the Broncos offense finally stirred to life thanks to a 55-yard touchdown run from Phillip Lindsay. Lock then threw fourth-quarter touchdown passes to Albert Okwuegbunam and DaeSean Hamilton to bring the Broncos within touching distance.

A one-yard touchdown connection from Lock to K. J. Hamler tied the score as time expired, with Brandon McManus converting the PAT to give the Broncos a highly improbable victory.

4. Son of Bum Returns

It's common enough to see an assistant coach learn the ropes, head elsewhere as a coordinator, then return to his original team in a head coaching capacity. Take

Mike Shanahan and Gary Kubiak, for example (and you'll find plenty about them elsewhere in the book). It's much rarer for a one-time head coach to return to his former team as a coordinator.

"Son of Bum" was fired as Broncos head coach with a middling 16-16 record following two seasons in charge in the 1990s. After spells in Buffalo, Atlanta, San Diego, and Houston, Phillips returned to the Mile High City in 2015 as a coordinator and masterminded one of the greatest defensive seasons in NFL history.

Combine a smart, dynamic, and aggressive bunch of players with Phillips' all-out attacking system and there was the potential for magic. And much magic did ensue, culminating in the complete domination of the No. 1 ranked Carolina Panthers offense in Super Bowl 50.

Phillips spent just one more season with the Broncos before being ousted in somewhat controversial circumstances. Short-lived his second spell in Denver might have been, but that amazing 2015 defense means that his legacy in Broncos Country is assured.

3. Peyton Manning's 2012 Season

A decade on, it's easy to look back at the Peyton Manning era and assume that it was always going to be a slam dunk. Success was anything but guaranteed, though. Manning had missed the whole of the 2011 season after all. Any injury that forces a player to miss a year is an extremely serious one. Especially if it's a neck injury and you're a quarterback.

Manning was so concerned about his lack of arm strength during rehab that he limited who could watch him throw. Speaking on the HBO show *On the Record with Bob Costas*, Manning admitted, "I was very sensitive to who could see me. I really only threw the football during that time, Bob, with about three people. With my wife — I let her see me throw — Eli and my dad. And that was it because I didn't want anyone else to see me and to see the reaction on their faces."[28]

Not exactly what you want to hear if you've gone all in on a quarterback. Thankfully for the Broncos, the hours of rehab paid off and Manning version 2.0 was even better than the original Colts incarnation. So successful was Manning's first season in Denver that he was named the NFL's Comeback Player of the Year. He remains the only Bronco to win that award. It wasn't all plain sailing in the first few weeks, though. Which brings us to this amazing matchup.

2. Broncos Overturn a Franchise Record 24-point Deficit to Beat Chargers

The Manning era in Denver got off to a rather sketchy start. After five games, the Broncos had a 2-3 record. Things weren't looking too clever at halftime of Week 6 either with the visitors staring a 24-0 deficit in the face against Norv Turner's Chargers.

The Broncos received the second-half kickoff and drove 85 yards, culminating in a 29-yard toss from Manning to Demaryius Thomas. On the following San Diego possession, Philip Rivers was sacked by Elvis Dumervil with Tony Carter taking the ensuing fumble to the house for a 65-yard touchdown. 24-14. Game on.

The defense forced a quick three-and-out before Manning led another TD drive, with this time Eric Decker finding the end zone. A Rivers interception was turned into a Denver lead courtesy of a 21-yard Brandon Stokley touchdown and the comeback was completed courtesy of a Chris Harris Jr. pick-six.

With those 35 unanswered points the Broncos were truly up and running. The franchise-record comeback marked the start of an 11-game winning streak, which was cruelly ended by the Ravens in the Division Round of the playoffs.

1. Terrell Davis' Migraine Miracle

"If you want the rainbow, you gotta put up with the rain." Wise words from country queen Dolly Parton. At Super Bowl XXXII, a deluge of virtual rain dropped on the head of Terrell Davis in the form of a crushing migraine in the second quarter.

After a stellar opening stanza that included 64 yards and a touchdown, Davis was temporarily blinded and forced to sit out most of quarter number two.

Speaking with Fox Sports' Mike Hill, Davis recalled the terrifying moment. "Nothing is clear, everything is in pieces. I just remember in my mind saying, 'No, no, no, not right now.'"[29]

Thankfully for the Broncos, Davis was good to go in the second half. An offense that had sputtered without their talismanic running back roared to life on the back of the eventual MVP. Davis ended up with 157 yards and three touchdowns and was the key element in the Broncos winning their maiden Lombardi Trophy. As Dolly might say, "That's quite the rainbow."

Trivia Test

In which round of the 2019 NFL Draft did the Broncos select quarterback Drew Lock?

a) First

b) Second

c) Third

Top 5 Celebrations

There are few more exhilarating feelings for a sports fan than watching your team score a crucial touchdown. You can feel the burst of energy flow through the stadium. If it's like that for the crowd, imagine what it's like for the players on the field. It's no wonder they want to strut their stuff following a big play. Here are five of the best Broncos celebrations.

5. Tebowing

The man himself said that his "celebration" wasn't actually a "celebration." For Broncos Country and the watching NFL public, it certainly looked like one. We are, of course, talking about Tim Tebow and his kneeling pose following a score.

"I never did it to celebrate a touchdown," Tebow told *USA Today* in 2018. "I did it from my sophomore year in high school all the way through the NFL, that before and after games I would get on a knee to thank my Lord and savior, Jesus Christ, and also put things into perspective. It was never something I did to take away from somebody else."[30]

"Tebowing" became something of an international phenomenon during the wild 2011 season with people dropping on one knee in a host of unusual situations. Check out Tebowing.com to see just how widespread (but short-lived) the move became.

4. Gerald Willhite's Back Flips

Gerald Willhite enjoyed a solid rather than spectacular career with the Broncos after being selected with the 21st overall pick in the 1982 NFL Draft.

The Stanford grad spent seven seasons in Denver and was an integral performer on the Dan Reeves-era teams, which reached Super Bowls XXI and XXII. As well as being a speedy rusher, Willhite was a real pass-catching threat. That's evident from his career receiving yards (1,767), which are higher than his career rushing yards (1,688). Not bad numbers for someone who didn't even play football in high school.

Willhite scored 22 touchdowns during his career and is best known throughout Broncos Country for the outrageous back flip celebration that followed many of them.

After retiring from football, Willhite went on to open his own restaurant, GW Spices BBQ in California.

3. Von Miller's X-Rated Sack Dance

Von Miller had a big personality to go with his oversized talent, and that flamboyance was on show each time he delivered a quarterback sack. The Broncos legend liked to mix up his moves, scoring highly for both technique and artistic impression.

The future Hall of Famer's most infamous move came following a sack in a 2015 game against the Chiefs. After taking Alex Smith to the ground, Miller celebrated with a hip-thrusting maneuver based on a skit by comedians Key & Peele.

Social media went wild but the NFL suits were less impressed, giving Miller an $11,567 fine for "unsportsmanlike conduct."

#58 wasn't put off, though, repeating the move and adding a little something extra in the form of a crotch grab after taking down Tom Brady in the 2015 AFC Championship Game. This move earned him a $23,152 fine.

The star pass rusher put plenty of thought into his moves. He told the media in October 2017, "Sack dances are for when you're just killing them. Okay, it's over. But you really don't want to get sack dances on first or second down. It doesn't matter how great the sack dance is.... If you get sacks on like second down and you dance and bust out a move and then they get the first down on the next play, you look like an idiot."[31]

Von showed off his dancing props in a more formal setting by appearing in the hit TV show *Dancing with the Stars*. Scoring highly for his Viennese Waltz, Miller finished seventh in 2016.

2. Sammy Winder's Mississippi Mud Walk

Grinding Sammy Winder was the Broncos' featured back for much of the 1980s. He might not have been the flashiest runner to wear orange, but if the o-line gave him just a crack to run through, you can bet your boots that Winder would find it. That hard-running style made him a big favorite with the Mile High crowd.

In his nine seasons in Denver, the 1982 fifth-round pick rushed for 5,427 yards, which is still good for third on the all-time list behind Terrell Davis and Floyd Little. The Southern Miss alum also scored 48 TDs, which offered plenty of opportunities to show off his signature celebration – The Mississippi Mud Walk – a sort of high-kicking wander through the end zone.

A key component in the successful teams of the mid-1980s, Winder went to the Pro Bowl in both 1984 and 1986.

1. The Mile High Salute

After the shock loss to the Jaguars that ended the 1996 season, Terrell Davis was looking for a spark at the 1997 training camp. He found it in the profession that he respected the most – the military. And with that, the Mile High Salute was born. It was a celebration that became a phenomenon as Davis became the game's dominant player and the Broncos the NFL's dominant team.

The Salute wasn't dragged out for any old play either. It was only allowed when the team scored a touchdown. What began in training camp made it all the way to two Super Bowl triumphs.

Speaking to the *Denver Post*'s Nicki Jhabvala prior to his induction into the Pro Football Hall of Fame, Davis expanded on the origin story.

"It was just simply a sign of respect," he said. "It was just my appreciation for service men and women, and I always thought the mentality that you have to have to play the running back position, you got to have the same mentality as a soldier. So I adopted that salute as the thing that I would do to my teammates, to the running backs, as a sign of respect when I scored."[32]

Trivia Test

Von Miller isn't the only Bronco to have appeared on the TV show *Dancing with the Stars*. Which twinkle-toed star was on the show in 2018?

a) Terrell Davis

b) Shannon Sharpe

c) DeMarcus Ware

Top 5 Trick Plays

One of the ultimate risk/reward maneuvers in pro football is the trick play. Time it right and execute it to perfection and it can make a coach look like a genius. Get it wrong, though, and it can make the coach look very silly indeed. The Broncos have enjoyed some spectacular successes when they've delved deep into the playbook for something a little funky. Here are the Top 5 Trick Plays.

5. Jim Turner vs. the Raiders

Up 14-7 on the road against the defending Super Bowl champion Oakland Raiders, Broncos head coach Red Miller decided to go for the jugular.

Lined up for a 42-yard field goal try, holder Norris Weese collected the snap and kicker Jim Turner performed a convincing fake kick before peeling off to the left of the line of scrimmage. Weese's original target was reliable receiver Riley Odoms, but seeing Turner in acres of space, he tossed the pass to his kicker.

The 36-year-old Turner made the grab and then ambled to the end zone for a 32-yard touchdown, the only one in his 16-year NFL career.

Helped by a rampant Denver defense, which intercepted Oakland quarterback Kenny Stabler seven times (!), the Broncos went on to rout the Raiders by a score of 30-7.

Not exactly an athlete in the prime of his career, Turner told reporters after the game, "I ran into the end zone out of fear. Speed wasn't involved."[33]

The Raiders' rout was a statement win in what proved to be a fantastic season for the Broncos.

4. Sanders to Sutton

There wasn't a huge amount to cheer for during the Vance Joseph era. One of the few rays of sunshine in a gloomy couple of seasons was a spectacular win against the Cardinals in 2018. The Broncos had lost four straight heading into their Week 7 trip to the desert. They saved their best performance of the season for this nationally televised Thursday Night contest, dismantling the Cardinals by a score of 45-10.

The game's undoubted MVP was Emmanuel Sanders. Not only did he catch six passes for 102 yards and a 64-yard touchdown, he also threw his first career touchdown pass.

Taking an end-around from quarterback Case Keenum, Sanders tossed a deep ball into the end zone. The ball was slightly overthrown, but Courtland Sutton made a spectacular diving grab to give the Broncos a 14-0 first-quarter lead.

3. Elway's Flea Flicker

Vance Johnson was a favorite target for John Elway. Only Shannon Sharpe caught more touchdown passes from #7 than the 1985 second-round pick. Not many were as intricate as the Elway-to-Johnson connection against the Seahawks in Week 8 of the 1986 season.

Elway took the snap and handed it off to Sammy Winder, who peeled right. Winder handed it to Steve Sewell, who tossed it back to Elway who lobbed a bomb toward the end zone. The Seattle defense wasn't really fooled, and the coverage was tight, but Johnson made a terrific catch for a memorable 34-yard touchdown.

Elway and Johnson combined for 32 touchdowns, but none were quite as spectacular as this superbly executed flea flicker.

2. Elway's Touchdown Catch

The Broncos opened the 1986 season with a home game against the Raiders. The three previous times the teams had met the game had gone to overtime. This one was expected to be close too, and it didn't disappoint.

The script wasn't exactly going to plan for the Broncos as the visitors jumped out to a 19-7 lead early in the second quarter. Not renowned for expansive play calling, Dan Reeves went into his bag of tricks to give the home team a spark while facing a third-and-six deep in Raiders territory.

Elway took a shotgun snap and delivered an inside handoff to Steve Sewell, who peeled right, abruptly stopped, and looked left. In his sights was Elway, who had snuck out of the backfield into space. #7 caught the perfectly delivered pass and rumbled into the end zone untouched for the touchdown. The Broncos went on to win a shootout 38-36 courtesy of a seven-yard Elway pass to Gene Lang in the fourth quarter.

The 23-yard grab would prove to be Elway's only career receiving touchdown.

1. Run, Peyton, Run

This might not technically qualify as a trick play, but it certainly fooled the broadcasters, the opposition, the fans, and pretty much everyone. Peyton Manning had many, many fantastic qualities as a quarterback. Running was not one of them. Usain Bolt he ain't. In 85 games for the Broncos, Manning had a total of minus-55 rushing yards. #18 managed just a single rushing touchdown during his time in Denver, but it was an absolute doozy.

Facing a third-and-goal from the one with 52 seconds left in the first half in a 2013 visit to Dallas, the Broncos were looking to build on a 21-17 lead. The visitors beefed up their power formation by bringing in defensive lineman Mitch Unrein as fullback. As tight end Julius Thomas motioned behind the line, a run up the middle by Knowshon Moreno looked a certainty.

Instead, Manning delivered a perfect fake and, with all eyes on the pile, bootlegged untouched into the corner of the end zone for a fantastic score.

Despite Cowboys quarterback Tony Romo throwing for 506 yards and five touchdowns, the Broncos won 51-48 courtesy of a Matt Prater field goal as time expired.

Trivia Test

Which Broncos receiver threw 81- and 30-yard touchdown passes in 1992 and 1993 games against the Cowboys and Colts?

a) Mark Jackson

b) Arthur Marshall

c) Cedric Tillman

Top 5 Players with Colorado Connections

It's great to see a player with local roots do well in their football career. Especially if that success takes place on home territory. The Broncos have benefited from a number of "hometown heroes." Here are the top five players with Colorado connections.

5. Tyler Polumbus

There was a satisfying symmetry to the NFL career of Tyler Polumbus. The former Colorado Buffalo signed with the Broncos as an undrafted free agent in 2008 and quickly made his mark. The Denver native appeared in all 16 games in his rookie season and won the starting guard job a year later.

Waived in 2010, Polumbus bounced around the league with spells in Detroit, Seattle, Washington, and Atlanta.

After an injury to former Colorado State Ram Ty Sambraillo in October 2015, the Broncos turned to the familiar figure of Polumbus. Adding depth to a banged-up line, the Cherry Creek High School alum appeared in 11 games and won himself an unexpected Super Bowl ring.

Polumbus went out at the top, that Super Bowl being his last appearance as a pro. He's remained in Colorado post-retirement, becoming a familiar figure on local sports radio.

4. Shaq Barrett

Von Miller and DeMarcus Ware were the headline pass-rushing attractions on the all-conquering 2015 Super Bowl-winning team. They weren't the only threats to the health of opposition quarterbacks, though. Shaq Barrett had his moments too.

The Colorado State Ram joined the Broncos as an undrafted free agent in 2014 and added depth to an already stacked defense. Filling in for the injured DeMarcus Ware, Barrett made it count in his first NFL start. A stat sheet in the 2015 Week 6 encounter against Cleveland that included 1.5 sacks, nine tackles, and a forced fumble gave notice that the Broncos had another serious talent on their hands.

The former CSU star didn't look back, gaining plenty of playing time throughout the season, culminating in the 2015 Super Bowl win over the Panthers.

With starting opportunities limited in Denver, Barrett signed with the Bucs in 2019. The Florida move has been a profitable one as Barrett delivered a league-best 19.5 sacks in his first season and followed it up by winning a second career Super Bowl ring in 2021.

3. Rick Dennison

Another CSU linebacker to enjoy a successful career in Denver was Rick Dennison. Younger readers might only recognize the name as the coordinator of some rather vanilla offenses in the mid-2010s. There's much more to "Rico" than that.

The undrafted linebacker spent nine seasons with the Broncos from 1982, helping the team to three AFC championships. After hanging up his cleats in 1990 the

Rocky Mountain High School alum picked up a coaching clipboard and started a successful second half to his career.

After spells as offensive line coach, special teams coach, and offensive coordinator, Dennison was reunited with former teammate Gary Kubiak, who named him the OC with the Houston Texans. The pair then headed to Baltimore before returning to Denver for a second spell in 2015.

After the pyrotechnics of the early Peyton Manning era, the final season with #18 running the show wasn't quite as spectacular. Reflecting the physical limitations of their aging quarterback, the Kubiak/Dennison offense put far greater emphasis on the running game. It didn't have the flair of previous years, but in combination with a dazzling defense, it got the job done.

After departing Denver in 2016, Dennison got the OC gig in Buffalo and later served as a senior offensive assistant with the Minnesota Vikings.

2. Phillip Lindsay

Broncos Country loves a trier. Especially one who's a hometown kid. Scrappy, tenacious, and all-effort, Phillip Lindsay quickly became a fan favorite with Mile High crowds.

The Broncos have Lindsay's mother to thank for him playing in Denver. After being overlooked in the 2018 NFL Draft, Lindsay received a number of offers, but Mom Diane recommended that the former Buffalo stay home. It proved to be a wise move as Lindsay enjoyed a stellar rookie season.

Lindsay rushed for 1,037 yards at a hugely impressive average of 5.4 yards per carry in that first season. Add 35 catches plus a total of 10 touchdowns into the mix and it's easy to see how Lindsay became the first undrafted rookie running back to receive Pro Bowl recognition. Another 1,000-yard season followed a year later.

It was Lindsay's feisty attitude that endeared him to Broncos Country as much as the numbers. He might not have had the stature of some players, but he had plenty of game and was never one to back down from confrontation.

There have been few bright spots in the post-Manning era. Phillip Lindsay's play was one of them.

1. Alfred Williams

A captain on the 1990 national championship-winning Colorado Buffaloes team, Alfred Williams "came home" to Denver in 1996 and added even more silverware to his collection.

"Big Al" spent the first four seasons of his pro career in Cincinnati after being selected 18th overall in the first round of the 1991 NFL Draft. After a brief stop in San Francisco, the defensive lineman returned to the Centennial State in 1996, making a huge impression in his first year in orange and blue. That 13-sack season was good enough to earn the pass rusher both Pro Bowl and First-Team All-Pro honors.

Williams didn't quite match those eye-popping numbers in the years that followed but still had a big play or two in him. Two sacks in the tight 1997 Divisional Round playoff win at Kansas City are a case in point.

Combining superbly with Neil Smith and Maa Tanuvasa, the one-time Buff would go on to add two Super Bowl rings to his national championship.

After retiring from football in 1999, Williams remained in the Denver area forging a career as a radio broadcaster, first on KKFN and now on KOA, where he co-hosts the drivetime "Sports Zoo" show.

Trivia Test

Colorado-born defensive lineman Ben Garland was a member of which branch of the US military?

a) Air Force

b) Army

c) Navy

Top 5 Big Man Touchdowns

It's great when the big guys get their moment of glory. Who doesn't enjoy watching a burly lineman rumble down the field, ball in hand, making a long fumble or interception return? Here are five of the best Big Man touchdowns that Broncos Country has enjoyed.

5. Trevor Pryce vs. the Raiders

Any touchdown against the Raiders is welcome. Even better if it's on the road and comes from a defensive player. Trevor Pryce managed to do just that in a September 2000 game at the Oakland Coliseum.

After an Ed McCaffrey touchdown midway through the first quarter gave the visitors a 7-0 lead, the Broncos doubled their advantage on the Raiders' first play from scrimmage. Quarterback Rich Gannon was hit and fumbled. Pryce made the recovery and romped into the end zone untouched to score a 28-yard touchdown.

It was a lead the Broncos held for the rest of the game as Mike Anderson rushed for 189 yards, Brian Griese threw a second touchdown pass to Howard Griffith, and the defense picked off Gannon twice and sacked him four times.

Pryce, a 1997 first-round pick, was a superb addition for the Broncos. In nine seasons, the former Clemson star registered 325 tackles, two interceptions, and 64 sacks. The Raiders fumble rumble was his only career touchdown.

4. Mitch Unrein vs. Tampa Bay, 2012

Peyton Manning shared the love when it came to touchdown passes with the Broncos. No fewer than 16 different Denver receivers caught at least one touchdown pass from #18, even defensive linemen. The lineman in question was big Mitch Unrein.

Sometimes used as a fullback on short yardage and goal line plays, the man from Eaton, Colorado got his name on the scoresheet in a December 2012 game against the Bucs. On a first-and-goal play from the Tampa Bay one-yard line, Unrein peeled to the left of the end zone and caught a gently lobbed Manning pass to give the Broncos a 7-0 lead.

That game against the Bucs was arguably the best of Unrein's career. Late in the third quarter, he delivered a big hit on Tampa Bay quarterback Josh Freeman that resulted in a pick, which was returned by Von Miller for a 26-yard score.

A 100% catch percentage, a 100% scoring percentage, and the first Broncos defensive lineman to score an offensive touchdown are pretty good records to have.

3. Neil Smith vs. Miami, 1998 Divisional Round playoff

The Broncos' 1998 Divisional Round playoff win over the Dolphins was one of the most complete performances in franchise history. The exclamation point on the 38-3 rout came in the form of a classic "Big Man Touchdown" courtesy of pass rusher Neil Smith.

Denver cornerback Darrius Johnson forced a fumble from Miami receiver Oronde Gadsden midway through the fourth quarter, which Smith scooped up at the Broncos' 21-yard line. A couple of crunching blocks later and the defensive end was away, racing – not especially quickly, it has to be said – up the left sideline for a 79-yard touchdown.

The touchdown was just Smith's second in 11 seasons and the first in Broncos colors.

2. Keith Traylor vs. Buffalo, 1997

Keith Traylor had a very interesting career, morphing from a 260-pound linebacker into a 332-pound defensive tackle behemoth. It was while assuming the latter role that he enjoyed his most spectacular play as a Bronco.

During the Broncos' visit to Buffalo in 1997, a game that almost didn't happen thanks to an enormous blizzard in Denver (see the Top 5 Weather Games for more), Traylor scored his first career touchdown, and it was a beauty.

Leading 13-0 in the third quarter, the sure-handed Traylor picked off a Todd Collins pass and took off down the sideline. Showing excellent speed for a man his size and some very nifty footwork, the defensive lineman ambled home for a 62-yard touchdown.

The Bills rallied in the fourth quarter to tie the game at 20-20, but a Jason Elam field goal in overtime sealed the deal for a statement road win.

1. Malik Jackson, Super Bowl 50

You'd have got long odds on the first touchdown of Super Bowl 50 being scored by Malik Jackson. Demaryius Thomas, Emmanuel Sanders, or C. J. Anderson perhaps, but Malik Jackson? Given how dominant the Denver defense had been throughout the whole of the 2015 season, it's perhaps not that surprising that the opening touchdown of Super Bowl 50 was scored by a defensive tackle.

Facing a third-and-10 from their own 15 midway through the first quarter, Panthers quarterback Cam Newton dropped back to pass. A rampant Von Miller burst through the line, smothered Newton, and stripped the ball, which wobbled into the end zone. DeMarcus Ware had a shot at it, but it was Malik Jackson who fell on the ball to score his only career touchdown and give the Broncos a crucial 10-0 lead.

It doesn't score highly in terms of style points, but there's been no more important "Big Man Touchdown" than the one Malik Jackson scored at Super Bowl 50.

Trivia Test

In what country was former defensive end Harald Hasselbach born?

a) Denmark

b) Germany

c) The Netherlands

Top 5 Talkers

Being susceptible to trash talking was described by gritty Australian cricket captain Steve Waugh as a form of "mental disintegration." Can a timely comment get under the skin of your opponent and force them into a mistake? The Broncos have had some masters of these dark arts. They've also had some comedians whose chatter has delivered plenty of laughs. Here are the Top 5 Talkers.

5. Dave Logan – "Here We Go"

He may have only caught a single pass in Denver colors, but there's no voice more associated with the Broncos than Dave Logan's. The longtime Cleveland Browns receiver moved to the KOA radio commentary booth in 1990, firstly as a color announcer, then shifted to the play-by-play chair in 1996 and has been there ever since.

Part of an exclusive club of athletes drafted by NFL, NBA, and MLB teams (Dave Winfield and Mickey McCarty are the others), Logan has made the call on many of the greatest moments in franchise history.

The former Buff has also excelled as a high school head coach, leading his teams to a host of Colorado state championship titles.

There are three magical words that Broncos Country wants to hear whenever Logan has the mic – "Here We Go." That usually means that something good is just about to happen.

4. Aqib Talib – Don't Wear a Chain

The No Fly Zone was one of the most dominant secondaries in the history of the NFL. Most of the time they could let their play do the talking. Sometimes, though, there was some smack to be dished out, usually from Aqib Talib.

Shy and *retiring* are not words that you would use to describe the former New England Patriot who was the most vocal presence on the dominant Broncos defense of the mid-2010s. Just ask Oakland's Michael Crabtree.

The pair, both of whom hail from Dallas, had previously clashed in a matchup between Tampa Bay and San Francisco. The beef really exploded during the 2016 season finale between the Broncos and Raiders when Talib grabbed Crabtree's chain and snatched it from his neck.

The teams met again in November 2017, and it didn't take long for simmering tensions to boil over. Some overenthusiastic blocking from the Raiders receiver prompted an enormous brawl, which resulted in multiple punches being thrown, flags appearing like confetti on a wedding day, and both players being ejected.

The feuding Texans kissed and made up in rather bizarre circumstances, after bumping into each other at a go-kart track. Realizing how ridiculous the spat had gotten, the pair shook hands and decided to call time on one of the league's most notorious beefs.[34]

3. Tom Jackson – "It's All Over, Fat Man"

The Broncos and Raiders were founded in the same year, 1960. It's fair to say that the Silver and Black found their feet much quicker than their Mile High rivals. By 1976 the Raiders had won nine division titles, appeared in the AFL/AFC Championship eight times, and won a Super Bowl. In that 16-year period, the

Broncos had never reached the playoffs, never won a division title, and only managed three winning seasons.

To say they had an inferiority complex against the Raiders is something of an understatement. Consider that from 1963 to 1976 the teams met 30 times and the Broncos won just two of them. Two!

The footballing equivalent of the playground bully would get their comeuppance in 1977. Thanks to a dominant performance by the Orange Crush defense that picked off seven passes, and one of the best trick plays in franchise history, the Broncos delivered a 30-7 road upset of the defending Super Bowl champions.

Nobody exemplified the Broncos' newfound swagger than linebacker Tom Jackson, yelling "It's all over, fat man!" at Raiders coach John Madden. There was a new kid on the AFC West block and the NFL had better watch out.

Jackson moved from the field to the studio after hanging up his cleats, becoming a popular ESPN pundit. His famous quote against the Raiders was the sign that the Broncos had come of age.

2. Mark Schlereth – The Stinkin' Truth

As well as being an all-time great position group, the 1990s Broncos offensive line were noted for their lack of enthusiasm when dealing with the media. "Silence is golden" could have been their motto. Unusual then that one of their number has gone on to become one of the NFL's most prominent talkers.

We're talking, of course, about the multi-talented Mark Schlereth. Not content with winning three Super Bowls, "Stink" has enjoyed a varied post-playing career that has included creating a brand of chili sauce alongside a host of media gigs.

After a spell hosting the *Drive Time Show* on 760 The Zone, listeners in Denver can tune into Schlereth (and Mike Evans) on the *Breakfast Show* on 104.3 The Fan.

The longtime Broncos guard is the regular wingman of play-by-play announcer Adam Amin on Fox's televised NFL broadcasts. You can also hear his opinions on *The Stinkin' Truth Podcast*. The Alaska-born lineman has even had a crack at acting, making regular appearances in the TV soap *Guiding Light*.

That's quite the media resume for a man whose postgame routine usually consisted of a brief "no comment."

1. Shannon Sharpe – "We need the National Guard…"

Shannon Sharpe is one of the loudest, most opinionated pundits on the NFL media circuit. He wasn't shy about voicing an opinion or two during his playing career either. The trash talking was all part of a superb all-round package, and Sharpe put it to savage use on occasions.

Take, for example, the time he managed to get Kansas City's Hall of Fame pass rusher Derrick Thomas to commit three personal foul penalties. What was the cause of this mental meltdown? Sharpe had reportedly got hold of the phone number of Thomas' girlfriend and was repeating it at the line of scrimmage. All this as the Broncos were compiling an 80-yard touchdown drive during a 30-7 road rout at Arrowhead in November 1998. Amazingly, 75 of those 80 yards came courtesy of Kansas City penalties.

"I have perfected the talent to make people upset. Trust me. I know what to say to get to anybody," Sharpe told reporters after the game. [35]

Sharpe's most famous "talkie" came during another road rout, this time of the Patriots in 1996. On the back of a three-touchdown effort from Terrell Davis, the Broncos had a huge lead at Foxboro, which prompted Sharpe to pick up the phone.

"Mr. President. We need the National Guard! We need as many men as you can spare because we are killing the Patriots!"[36]

Caught by a well-placed sideline camera, Sharpe's call was rated #46 in the NFL's Top 50 Sound FX.

Talking the talk is all well and good but counts for little if you can't also walk the walk. Shannon Sharpe could undoubtedly do both.

Trivia Test

Shannon Sharpe got involved in a heated on-court row with members of which team during a 2023 NBA game?

a) Memphis Grizzlies

b) New York Knicks

c) Philadelphia 76ers

Top 5 Individual Player Nicknames

A sure sign that you've made it as an NFL player is being given a nickname. Broncos players have been christened with some magnificent and memorable monikers. Here are the Top 5 Individual Player nicknames.

5. Rich Jackson – Tombstone

A defensive end whose nickname was "Tombstone" was always likely to put the fear of God in offensive linemen, and Rich Jackson most certainly did.

Acquired via a trade with the Raiders in 1967, Jackson started 67 games for the Broncos, registering an impressive 43 sacks. His signature move is the now outlawed "head slap," or as Jackson himself described it, the "halo spinner."

The first Bronco to receive All-Pro honors and an original addition to the Ring of Fame, "Tombstone" also went to three Pro Bowls during his six seasons in Denver. A knee injury cut short his career in Colorado, and he spent a brief spell in Cleveland before retiring.

Interviewed in 1968, Jackson said his chosen style of play was "an aggressive style. I like to hit people and I like to go hard."[37]

Which is just what you want to hear from your premier pass rushing threat.

4. Mark Schlereth – Stink

There are two theories as to how Mark Schlereth got his unforgettable nickname of "Stink." The more prosaic answer is that the former guard was partial to a fish dish called "Stinkman" favored by the Eskimo population in his native Alaska. Hmm... The second explanation is far more interesting.

Sometimes, you've just got to go. Even if you're in the middle of a football field with millions of viewers watching. Schlereth figured everyone was looking at John Elway rather than him so why not let it all out.

A nickname based on peeing your pants might be a bit gross, but it's been a marketing masterstroke for the longtime mainstay of the Broncos offensive line. *The Stinkin' Truth* is a great name for a podcast. As is Stinkin' Good Green Chile.

A media personality coming from an offensive line that famously refused to speak to the media seemed unlikely. Even more so is a media personality whose nickname is based on a bodily function. Schlereth's larger-than-life personality has won the day, though.

3. Karl Mecklenburg – The Albino Rhino/Snow Goose

You don't often find treasure in the lower reaches of the NFL Draft, but the Broncos discovered a diamond when they picked Karl Mecklenburg in Round 12 in 1983.

Mecklenburg became the focal point of a Broncos defense that was a perennial contender throughout the linebacker's time in Denver. He was also the holder of not one but two memorable nicknames.

Sometimes known as the "Snow Goose," #77's main moniker was "The Albino Rhino." There's no great backstory to the creation of the Albino Rhino nickname. Mecklenburg was simply called it by one of his friends at the University of Minnesota, who thought it a clever name for a fair-skinned, light-blond 240-pounder. The name stuck and followed him throughout his career and beyond. There's even an Albino Rhino-themed clothing range available if you fancy a Mecklenburg T-shirt or hoodie.

2. Terrance Knighton – Pot Roast

Usually weighing in at over 300 pounds, defensive linemen like tucking into a good dinner. That was certainly true of tackle Terrance Knighton, who enjoyed two successful years in Denver after a four-season spell in Jacksonville.

Affectionately known as "Pot Roast," the 335-pound Knighton was reunited with former Jags head coach Jack Del Rio in 2013, becoming a key piece in the team that made it all the way to Super Bowl XLVIII against Seattle. A sturdy presence against the run, "Pot Roast" also registered six sacks and an interception in his two seasons with the Broncos.

So where did Knighton's memorable moniker come from? The credit goes to Jacksonville linebacker Clint Ingram. The Jags were on a flight back from a road game in Seattle and most of the team members were getting some much-needed sleep. Not Knighton, though, especially when mealtime was approaching. When a stewardess walked down the aisle offering "pot roast," Knighton was keen to dig in. Ingram thought it was a perfect name for his teammate, and one of the NFL's all-time great nicknames was born.

1. Steve Atwater – The Smiling Assassin

Many of the NFL's toughest defenders have a distinct air of menace about them. It's hard to picture the likes of Ray Lewis, Jack Lambert, or James Harrison being anything but gruff and grumpy. You don't have to be mean to be a tough guy, though, and there's no better example than Steve Atwater.

He could hit as hard as anyone in the league but would often offer a smile while picking up an opponent who'd been crushed into the turf. The "Smiling Assassin" was the perfect description for the supremely talented safety.

Atwater gained his nickname at training camp in his rookie year courtesy of defensive backs coach Charlie Waters. "Every time he would knock the crap out of somebody in practice, he came up smiling," Waters explained in a 2019 interview with the *Denver Post*'s Patrick Saunders. "That's just who Steve was. He was such a happy player. He was a happy warrior."[38]

It took a while for Atwater to get used to his new sobriquet. "I thought it was kind of corny, to tell you the truth," Atwater told the *Denver Post*. "But then I kind of embraced it, because at that point in my career I appreciated anything they were going to call me."[39]

Trivia Test

"Chicken" was the nickname of which Broncos defensive back?

a) Tyrone Braxton

b) Dennis Smith

c) Louis Wright

Top 5 Post-Football Careers

Long gone are the days when a player would open up a bar or sporting goods store when they retired from the game. There are ample opportunities for former NFL stars to follow their dreams and do something different away from the gridiron. Here are five Broncos who have enjoyed unexpected post-football careers.

5. Elvis Dumervil – Real Estate

Elvis Dumervil made a very good career out of taking the opposition's most valuable property to the ground. In his post-playing career, he's been doing the opposite, building things up rather than crashing them down.

What started with a small building in Fort Lauderdale has developed into something of a property empire. Since launching Prestige Estates back in 2016, Dumervil has built up a portfolio of hundreds of rental units in the Miami area.

Raised in Miami, Dumervil wanted to give something back to the area he grew up in. It's not just about making a buck. The goal is to provide comfort and value as well as to create jobs in the neighborhood.

"We acquire properties and renovate them to the highest standard. Our goal is to increase the quality of living not only of our residents, but also our neighbors."[40]

4. Ed McCaffrey – Horseradish Sauce

What is it with Broncos players and condiments? Was there something missing from the hot dogs and burgers at Mile High? Mark Schlereth is the best-known purveyor of hot sauce via his Stinkin' Good Green Chile. "Stink's" former teammate from the double Super Bowl-winning teams, Ed McCaffrey, also sunk his teeth into the sauce business.

The former wide receiver launched a series of mustards and sauces including spicy brown, chipotle, horseradish, and sriracha flavors, all under McCaffrey's Rocky Mountain label.

It's just part of a wide-ranging post-playing career that has also included spells as a radio host, color commentator on Broncos radio broadcasts, football camp host, and college head coach.

3. Trevor Pryce – Author, TV Producer, and Animation Expert

Trevor Pryce enjoyed a superb career as a Bronco. The 28th overall pick in 1997 spent nine seasons in Denver, amassing 325 tackles, 64 sacks, and two interceptions. Four Pro Bowls and two Super Bowl rings represent an excellent return for this dominant defender.

After a successful spell in Baltimore and a brief stint with the Jets, Pryce focused on his other great loves away from football, writing and animation. Pryce's first young adult graphic novel, *Kulipari: An Army of Frogs*, was published in 2013 and adapted into an animated Netflix series in 2016.

Pryce later founded Outlook OVFX Enterprises, a Baltimore-based multimedia studio that produces animated content for streaming platforms including Nickelodeon and Netflix as well as mixing and post-production for the music industry.

Creativity, versatility, and a strong work ethic served Pryce superbly in Denver, and they've helped the former lineman develop a hugely impressive career away from the football field.

2. Rich Karlis – Woodworker

Rich Karlis was always something of a craftsman. There weren't many barefoot kickers left plying that very particular trade in the NFL in the 1980s. Karlis has swapped feet for hands in his most recent post-football career. After a lengthy spell in the corporate world, the former kicker has transferred to the workshop.

"Growing up in my father's business I fell in love with wood while sanding large gym floors. Nothing is more beautiful than a newly sanded gym floor."[41] Karlis has turned that love of working with wood into a successful artisan business.

Products available at the superbly named Barefoot Bronco Woodworking include beautifully handcrafted charcuterie boards, cutting boards, chess boards, and serving trays. Our favorites from the Karlis catalogue are the Barefoot Bronco drinks coasters, complete with the Colorado state logo.

1. Jake Plummer – Mushroom Farmer

Jake Plummer was a player who always trod his own unique path. How many quarterbacks would retire at 32, just a year after taking his team to a conference championship game, and leave over $5 million on the table. "The Snake" did just that, enjoying the quiet life, playing some handball, and driving for a Meals on Wheels program.

The former All-Pro's big passion these days is mushrooms. Yes, you read that right. Mushrooms. Plummer is a huge proponent of the potential medical benefits of the humble fungi.

The former quarterback is part of a group that set up the Mycolove Farm in Upton, Colorado, which grows and sells medicinal and culinary mushrooms. Mycolove's goal is "to build a lasting, trustworthy, dependable brand that offers the highest potency, full-fruit body medicine for your mind, body and soul."

Plummer is quite the evangelist for the benefits of mushrooms. He told CBS Colorado's Romi Bean, "As an athlete, I wish I had this knowledge back when I was playing. I think it would have helped me deal with stress and come out of the game a little less beat up and less zapped from the intensity of the environment I was living in for so long."

"It's a true gift given to me to spread the word to people who are interested and maybe tired of being sick and tired," Plummer added.[42]

Just like in his playing career, the unorthodox quarterback is truly walking to the beat of his own drum.

Trivia Test

Who was the last Bronco before Von Miller to register double-digit sacks in back-to-back seasons?

a) Elvis Dumervil

b) Simon Fletcher

c) Trevor Pryce

Top 5 Shocking Moments

Drama is something that has never been in short supply for the Denver Broncos. Looking back, that drama was often rather trivial. At times, though, it has been truly tragic. Here are the Top 5 Shocking Moments in franchise history.

5. Broncos Ditch the Orange Uniforms

No team in the NFL was more associated with their uniform color than the Denver Broncos. Which made it such a shock when the team unveiled jerseys for the 1997 season that were dominated by navy blue rather than orange.

Owner Pat Bowlen wanted a fresh, modern look for the team and turned to Nike for inspiration. Assistant designer Rick Bakas told The Athletic that Mr. B. had asked for "a horse that looks like it's going to kick your ass."[43]

The move wasn't hugely popular with fans or even some of the players. John Elway especially wasn't enamored with the new look: "I didn't like them just because they weren't orange."

One player who was pleased with the transformation, though, was free agent signee Neil Smith "I don't know if I ever could have worn that orange jersey. I like the new ones. They're thumbs up with me."[44]

Elway and Broncos Country would eventually come around to the blue jerseys. The star quarterback was a perfect 21-0 in games when he dressed in blue. And most famously of all, the Broncos broke their Super Bowl hoodoo wearing their natty new navy attire.

4. Shanny Gets Fired

With two Super Bowls in the bank, you'd think that Mike Shanahan was untouchable in Denver. Expectations were so high from owner Pat Bowlen that missing the playoffs for three straight seasons warranted the chop.

Boasting a three-game lead in the AFC West with three games remaining in the 2008 season, the Broncos collapsed, losing all three for an 8-8 record and another playoff whiff. That disastrous finish was enough for Bowlen to call time on his head coach.

The Broncos didn't tear it up during Shanny's final three years in Denver, not helped by some pretty awful draft picks. The 24-24 win-loss record put them in the middle of the NFL pack, but defensive frailties stopped them from becoming true contenders. They were always competitive, though.

Shanny had been part of the Denver furniture for so long it seemed unthinkable he'd leave. Imagine the Steelers firing Mike Tomlin, the Ravens John Harbaugh, or even the Patriots saying cheerio to Bill Belichick, and you get the picture.

3. Dwight Harrison Pulls a Gun on His Teammate

Football is such a physically demanding and highly adversarial game, there are always going to be confrontations between players. They usually take place on the field and with opponents, but occasionally things can get a little spicy among teammates.

One such occasion involved speedy receiver Dwight Harrison and rugged defensive lineman Lyle Alzado during a 1972 practice. The pair exchanged verbal barbs and then physical blows with the row leaving Harrison so angry, he threatened to kill Alzado.

All talk and bluster, his teammates assumed. Hmmmm. Hours later, Harrison returned to the practice facility brandishing a gun, demanding to know the whereabouts of Alzado. Running back Floyd Little and coach Lou Saban managed to talk the emotional Harrison down and get the gun without it being fired.

Harrison was traded to the Bills later that day. In return, the Broncos acquired the services of star receiver Haven Moses, so Harrison's head-loss moment proved beneficial for the Broncos in the end.

2. Romanowski Spits at J. J. Stokes

Losing the penultimate game of the 1997 regular season to San Francisco was bad enough. The 34-17 defeat was overshadowed by an incident that could have derailed the whole campaign.

After a confrontation between Bill Romanowski and the 49ers' J. J. Stokes, the Broncos linebacker spat in the face of his opponent. Caught on camera, the incident led to a media frenzy and a firestorm of criticism from all directions including from Romanowski's teammates.

Shannon Sharpe described the players' team meeting that followed the incident as "the most tense locker room situation" he experienced in the NFL.

Romanowski, who was fined $7,500, later apologized for the extremely ugly incident. "What I did was totally inexcusable. Sometimes when emotion is high, logic is low, and I did something that is totally unacceptable. I hold myself accountable for my actions. What I did was dead wrong and I'm sorry for it."[45]

1. The Death of Darrent Williams

There's been no event more shocking in the history of the Denver Broncos than the death of Darrent Williams. With an infectious personality and talent to burn, the youngster made a big impression on and off the field in his first two seasons and looked set for a stellar NFL career.

The popular cornerback was at a nightclub with a group of friends and teammates following a 26-23 overtime loss to the 49ers on New Year's Eve 2006. A confrontation developed with another group, reportedly after champagne had been sprayed over guests in the VIP section.

A further altercation followed outside the venue as Williams and his friends exited in a white Hummer limousine. Shots were fired at the Hummer from an SUV and Williams was hit, tragically dying in the arms of teammate Javon Walker. He was just 24.

Willie Clark was found guilty of murder in 2010 and was sentenced to life in prison.

The young defensive back's legacy lives on in Denver courtesy of the Darrent Williams Good Guy Award. Chosen by members of the local media, the award is given to the player who best exemplifies "enthusiasm, cooperation and honesty."

Trivia Test

In their first two seasons, what color home uniforms did the Broncos wear?

a) Blue and white

b) Orange and blue

c) Yellow and brown

Top 5 Feuds and Fallouts

In a game dominated by alpha personalities where the stakes are so high, frank exchanges of views are commonplace. That's fine and dandy, of course, as long as they don't get out of hand. And sometimes they do. Very publicly too. Here are the Top 5 Feuds and Fallouts to affect Broncos Country.

5. John Elway and Dan Reeves

Despite multiple playoff appearances, division titles, and AFC championships, the waters on the Broncos sidelines during the Dan Reeves/John Elway era were often surprisingly choppy.

The pair butted heads over the style of offense the Broncos used with Elway wanting to open up the rigid, methodical, but often successful Reeves system.

The tensions bubbled to the surface in an interview where the star quarterback admitted he rarely spoke to his head coach, describing him as aloof, autocratic, and inflexible. Ouch.

Reeves, who had by then been fired by Denver and taken the reins at the New York Giants, returned the compliment in an interview with *Sports Illustrated*, saying, "One of these days I hope he grows up. Maybe he'll mature sometime."[46]

Thankfully this pair of legendary Broncos managed to repair their relationship. Elway invited his former coach to his Hall of Fame induction ceremony in 2004. "Time heals everything. Those types of things, those little problems, you just can't let them linger. They add up. Bitterness is no way to go through life. There are absolutely no ill feelings on my part toward Dan."[47]

Elway spoke kindly following Reeves' death in 2022. "The football world lost a heckuva coach and man today in Dan Reeves.... As the head coach, Dan was tough but fair. I respected him for that. We may not have always seen eye to eye, but the bottom line is we won a lot of games together. Looking back, what I appreciate about Dan is how he gradually brought me along to help me reach my potential."[48]

4. Broncos Country and Phil Simms

The hearts of much of Broncos Country would sink when they discovered that the commentary for a game would come from Jim Nantz and Phil Simms. There was no reason to grumble about the play-by-play announcer, but the color analyst certainly raised the hackles from a section of the fan base.

Watching this one play out from across the pond, it was hard to work out what the problem was. Sure, Simms could be a bit annoying, but couldn't most color commentators? The accusation was that he was biased against the Broncos, perhaps because his son, quarterback Chris, was a bust in Denver. Doesn't every fan base think that commentators are biased against their team? I can confirm that every Premier League Soccer fanbase thinks exactly that (and don't even start on match officials).

A campaign to stop Simms calling Broncos games attracted more than 40,000 signatures. Fans eventually got their wish, with Tony Romo getting the CBS gig in 2017.

3. Mike Shanahan and the Raiders

Mike Shanahan's brief spell as head coach of the Raiders wasn't a happy one. It's fair to say the head coach and owner weren't ever singing from the same hymn sheet. After going 7-9 in his first year with the Silver and Black, Shanny was canned by Al Davis just four games into the 1989 season. Not only was Shanahan fired, he was reportedly stiffed on some $250,000 owed. So was birthed one of the NFL's most notorious feuds, one which the Broncos would benefit from hugely.

It took a few years, but Shanahan would get his revenge on Davis and the Raiders. After a successful stint as offensive coordinator under George Seifert at the 49ers, Shanahan got his second head coaching gig, and it was one that offered ample opportunities for payback.

In 28 games against the Raiders, Shanahan led the Broncos to a hugely impressive 21-7 win-loss record. All NFL wins are important, especially ones against a notorious division rival. The ones against Al Davis and the Raiders were among the sweetest of all during the Shanahan years.

2. Terry Bradshaw and John Elway

Four-time Super Bowl winner Terry Bradshaw wasn't impressed when John Elway decided that he wouldn't sign if drafted by the Baltimore Colts, describing it as a "slap in the face to the National Football League" in a 1983 interview.

The four-time Super Bowl winner added, "In my opinion, he's not the kind of guy you win championships with. He never did it when he was at Stanford. I don't think he'll do it in Denver, & personally, (I) don't care if he ever does it."[49] Ouch.

Bradshaw maintained that frosty attitude throughout virtually all of Elway's pro career. In a press conference prior to Super Bowl XXIV, Bradshaw described Elway as having had "it too easy. He's been babied and pampered."

The feeling was mutual. "He's been bashing me since I got in the league. He doesn't like the money I've made. He can stick it in his ear."[50]

Elway would have the last laugh with his fiercest critic. After his MVP performance in the Super Bowl XXXIII win over the Falcons, who was tasked with handing over the Vince Lombardi Trophy? None other than Terry Bradshaw.

1. Josh McDaniels and Seemingly Everyone (Especially Jay Cutler)

A new, unproven, and extremely young head coach needs to put his stamp on a franchise. That's perfectly understandable. There are ways to deliver that stamp, but falling out with your Pro Bowl quarterback probably isn't the best way to do so.

McDaniels might not have fancied building an offense around Jay Cutler, but trying to trade him to New England in exchange for…Matt Cassel…surely wasn't the answer. After relations between head coach and quarterback broke down completely, Cutler was traded and the Broncos got Kyle Orton.

The journeyman quarterback had his moments, helping McDaniels to a 6-0 start including a famous win over New England. The McDaniels experiment soon came a cropper, though, as the Broncos won just two of the following 10 games. The wheels came right off following a 3-9 start to the 2010 campaign and the young coach was shown the exit.

McDaniels might have known his Xs and Os but he was no genius in handling personalities. In a 2022 interview with Pro Football Talk, McDaniels described what went wrong during his tenure in Denver. "I didn't really know people and how important that aspect of this process, and maintaining the culture and building the team, was. And I failed, and I didn't succeed at it."[51]

Trivia Test

Up to the start of the 2023 season, who was the last quarterback to lead the Broncos to a win over the Kansas City Chiefs?

a) Case Keenum

b) Peyton Manning

c) Trevor Siemian

Top 5 Famous Fans

Players and coaches may come and go but the one constant for a sports team is the fans. The Broncos have one of the best fanbases in the whole of sports. Loud and loyal, Broncos Country makes the Mile High experience one of the most memorable in football. With a sprinkling of stardust from a celebrity or two, here are the Top 5 Famous Fans.

5. Rich "G-Man" Goins – Billboard Man

It was midway through the 1990 season. The Broncos had started slowly, boasting a 3-5 record at the halfway point. Denver radio host Rich "G-Man" Goins still had faith in the team, taking a bet with a San Diego station. If the Broncos lost their game to the Chargers, he'd broadcast his show from atop a billboard on Colefax Avenue.

The Broncos duly lost, and rather than just broadcasting his show from the billboard, bosses suggested that Goins live up there until the Broncos' next win. A few extra days would be a great stunt and offer plenty of publicity for the station. Unfortunately for the radio host, the Broncos went on one of the worst losing streaks in living memory.

The billboard and its unusual resident became one of Colorado's quirkier tourist sites, attracting a host of visitors, including John Elway. An overtime loss to the

Bears followed by a Thanksgiving drubbing in Detroit and division defeats to the Raiders and Chiefs extended Goins' unorthodox vacation.

Not even freezing weather or bouts of bronchitis and pneumonia could get Goins down from his perch prematurely. The vigil eventually ended after 33 days, 16 hours, 5 minutes, and 21 seconds when the Broncos defeated the Chargers 20-10 in Week 15.

Goins' escapades gained national attention with the broadcaster appearing on the TV show *To Tell the Truth*.

4. Kate Hudson

The Broncos have quite the Hollywood fan club. Don Cheadle and Tim Allen are among the followers of all things orange. Arguably the most high-profile Broncos supporter among the acting fraternity is Kate Hudson.

Best known for movies including *Almost Famous*, *How to Lose a Guy in 10 Days*, and *Bride Wars*, Hudson is a regular and very vocal Broncos fan, especially on social media.

Raised in Colorado, Hudson was interviewed on the *Today Show* brandishing a Broncos tattoo (temporary) on her shoulder. The star was one of the lucky few in Santa Clara for the Super Bowl 50 triumph over the Panthers.

Orange blood obviously runs in the family as Hudson's mother, famed actress Goldie Hawn, is also a keen Broncos fan.

3. The South Park Guys

Trey Parker and Matt Stone, the brains behind the hit animated comedy series *South Park*, have been Broncos fans for the long haul. The Colorado natives have seen it all – the good times and bad, the Super Bowl disasters as well as the trio of Super Bowl wins. Bandwagon jumpers they most certainly ain't.

The Broncos have made regular cameo appearances in *South Park* too, with Cartman even dreaming that John Elway was his dad. (But who hasn't had that dream?)

The team repaid that loyalty during the Covid-interrupted 2020 season. With fan numbers restricted to just 5,700 for the game against the Buccaneers, the Broncos placed 1,800 cardboard cutouts of characters from the show in the South Stand as well as a backdrop of the town itself.

The Broncos Foundation benefited from the stunt courtesy of a bumper donation from Comedy Central.

2. Chauncey Billups – Mr. Big Shot

Five-time NBA All-Star Chauncey Billups is a huge Broncos fan. The longtime Detroit Piston and now head coach of the Portland Trail Blazers was born in Denver and attended the city's George Washington High School.

He's followed the fortunes of the Broncos since the 1980s, and in an interview with Broncos TV, he described being "born with orange blood."[52]

Speaking to the *Denver Post*'s Benjamin Hochman in 2014, the former Colorado Buffalo described his earliest memories of the team. "When I really first started getting into it was Gerald Willhite, doing those backflips, and Sammy Winder, you know what I'm saying, people like that. Simon Fletcher, I saw him one day in my neighborhood growing up, at this little soul food restaurant. I already was a fan, but that just took it to another level. Seeing Simon Fletcher. I was so in awe."[53]

He might not have won an NBA title in his spell with the Nuggets, but Billups has had plenty to cheer about from his hometown football team.

1. Barrel Man

Excluding players and coaches, the most identifiable representation of the Denver Broncos has been a man dressed only in suspenders, cowboy boots, and an orange barrel. I am of course talking about the legendary "Barrel Man," aka Tim McKernan.

The "Barrel Man" phenomenon started with a $10 bet. McKernan's brother wagered that if his sibling wore a barrel to a 1977 game he'd appear on TV. He most certainly did and a legendary figure in NFL fandom was born.

McKernan was a feature in the stands for more than 30 years and worked his way through more than 20 different barrels throughout his career as a fan. In 2006, one barrel was sold on eBay for a cool $30,000.

The barrel wasn't just a gimmick to get fame. McKernan was a massive and extremely genuine fan of the Broncos. He was even invited to John Elway's Pro Football Hall of Fame Induction ceremony (in black tie rather than the barrel!).

McKernan called time on the barrel in 2007 and died two years later at the age of 69. One of Broncos Country's biggest personalities, he's sorely missed.

Trivia Test

What is the name of the horse statue that has stood over Broncos' stadiums since the mid-1970s?

a) Bucky

b) Mucky

c) Lucky

Top 5 Group Nicknames

Plenty of individuals have managed to get a notable nickname (see the Top 5 Player Nicknames for some of the best), but it's far harder for position groups or combinations of players to earn a suitable sobriquet. The Broncos have delivered some elite units and partnerships and they've come with noteworthy names attached. Here are the Top 5 Group Nicknames.

5. The M&M Connection

Extremely unusual circumstances brought Haven Moses to Denver. The Buffalo receiver arrived via a 1972 trade with Buffalo after Bronco Dwight Harrison threatened teammate Lyle Alzado with a gun (see Top 5 Shocking Moments for more on this wild story).

Moses was a contributor for the Broncos right from the start but really hit his stride when joined by quarterback Craig Morton. The M&M Connection was a constant deep threat as the Broncos won their first division title and reached their maiden Super Bowl.

There's no greater example of the explosiveness of the M&M Connection than the historic 1977 AFC Championship Game against the Raiders. The Broncos took an early lead courtesy of a 74-yard Morton to Moses connection, then iced the game when the pair combined for a 12-yard score in the fourth quarter.

When Broncos Country looks back at the best quarterback/wide receiver tandems, the M&M Connection usually sits somewhere near the top of the list.

4. Orange Hush

What better epithet for a position group that took a vow of silence (with the media at least) than one that combines a play on a classic Broncos Country nickname and the group's Trappist monk tendencies?

Get quoted in the press and the linemen would issue their brethren a fine. Likewise, if a photo appeared in print. Brian Habib got caught appearing on a radio show. A big no-no, which resulted in a $1,500 fine. During the 1997 Super Bowl-winning season, the group amassed self-imposed fines of some $20,000.

Backup lineman Harry Swayne explained the philosophy behind keeping schtum in an interview with the *Los Angeles Times*. "Our group credo has been, 'People come to watch John Elway and Terrell Davis and no one cares about us and let's keep it that way.'"[54]

With the NFL handing out fines of $10,000 per day to players who didn't fulfill media obligations in the run-up to Super Bowl XXXIII, the group renounced their blackout and started talking. Even O-line guru Alex Gibbs.

The legendary assistant gave a typically salty answer when quizzed by reporters before the game against the Packers, telling reporters, "I'm hoping I'll be so boring, you'll say, 'Why in the world are we talking to this guy?'...and then I can get back over in oblivion and do what I do."[55]

3. The Three Amigos

If the M&M Connection was the Broncos' premier passing threat in the late '70s, a decade later it was the Three Amigos who picked up that mantle.

The Three Amigos in question were Vance Johnson, Mark Jackson, and Ricky Nattiel, drafted by the Broncos in 1985, 1986, and 1987, respectively. Together, they combined for more than 12,000 receiving yards and 77 touchdowns in Broncos colors and were responsible for some of the most memorable moments in franchise history.

Jackson grabbed the five-yard touchdown catch that was the culmination of "The Drive," while Nattiel etched his name in the record books by scoring a 56-yard touchdown on the opening play of Super Bowl XXII against Washington. Only Shannon Sharpe caught more touchdown passes from John Elway than Vance Johnson.

So where did the Three Amigos nickname come from? Johnson explained the origin in a 2013 interview with the *Denver Post*'s Terry Frei. "We rented the movie *Three Amigos!* with Martin Short, Steve Martin, and Chevy Chase. "I said, 'Mark (Jackson), I have a great idea! If they think three white guys can be Three Amigos, there's no way three black guys can't be Three Amigos!'"[56] The name stuck, and a Broncos legend was born.

2. No Fly Zone

An all-time great position unit needs a nickname to match, and the 2015 Broncos defensive backfield got just that with the No Fly Zone. Take to the air at your peril against this elite group.

That 2015 defense could do it all. Ranked first in total yards allowed, the unit always seemed to come up big when the moment required, whether that was a sack, a forced fumble, or a pick. The bigger the moment, the better they got.

This defense was all about the team rather than the individual. That was evident in the nickname that emphasized the group rather than a single player's prowess. Coined by Chris Harris Jr., the No Fly Zone was one of the most dominant secondaries the NFL has ever seen.

Others have tried to make the name their own, but the No Fly Zone will always be associated with the Broncos and their Super Bowl 50 lineup.

1. Orange Crush

Inspired by a popular brand of soda, there was no more appropriate nickname for the suffocating Broncos defense of the late 1970s than the Orange Crush. Packed with dominant playmakers who made life truly miserable for opponents, the Orange Crush was instrumental in turning the Broncos from also-rans to serious contenders.

It's no surprise just how good the Broncos became when you look at the quality of players that lined up on the defensive side of the ball. Good luck facing a unit that included Randy Gradishar, Tom Jackson, Lyle Alzado, Paul Smith, Rubin Carter, Barney Chavous, and Louis Wright.

Orchestrated by coordinator Joe Collier, the 1977 Broncos allowed a miserly 10.6 points per game en route to Super Bowl XII. The ball-hawking group created 39 turnovers and were especially stingy against the run. Opponents averaged just 3.3 yards per carry and scored just five touchdowns throughout the whole regular season.

The Orange Crush might never have won a Super Bowl, but they transformed the franchise from a laughingstock into a formidable force to be reckoned with. The 2015 Broncos defense is the best in franchise history, but the 1970s Orange Crush is right behind them.

Trivia Test

Who was the only member of the Three Amigos selected in the first round of the NFL Draft?

a) Mark Jackson

b) Vance Johnson

c) Ricky Nattiel

Top 5 Broncos Who Should Be in the Hall of Fame

When you consider that the Broncos have been one of the most successful franchises in the history of the NFL, it's shocking to see just how few players who called Denver home have been inducted into the Hall of Fame. The list of inductees currently includes John Elway, Gary Zimmerman, Floyd Little, Shannon Sharpe, Terrell Davis, Champ Bailey, Pat Bowlen, Steve Atwater, John Lynch, DeMarcus Ware and Peyton Manning. Here are five more Broncos who deserve a gold jacket.

5. Louis Wright

There's much more to being a shutdown corner than speed. Don't get me wrong, Louis Wright was plenty quick enough, but he also had the smarts to complement the physical talent.

Coming in at six-two, 200 pounds, Wright was a quality tackler as well as an excellent cover man. A crucial member of the Orange Crush defense, Wright was one of the four cornerbacks named to the NFL's 1970s All-Decade team. Guess who the only member of the quartet is who's not been inducted into Canton?

The knock on Wright was that he only picked off 26 passes in 12 seasons. It's hard to intercept passes when your coverage is so good that opposition quarterbacks rarely throw the ball in your direction.

That sentiment was echoed by Hall of Fame quarterback Dan Fouts. In a 2016 interview with *Sports Illustrated*, the Chargers legend said, "As far as Louis Wright is concerned, yeah, I do think he qualifies as a Hall of Famer. For me, he was tough. He was in the mold of Mike Haynes and Mel Blount as big and really athletic corners. We had to shy away from him, and that was not easy because he was on their left side…our right side…and it seems like you throw more passes to that side of the field. Anyway, I'd recommend him, no question."[57]

Who am I to argue with an all-time great quarterback?

4. Tom Nalen

The Broncos under Mike Shanahan were one of the best running teams the NFL has ever seen. Scheme certainly played a part, but you can't execute that scheme without the right players. And in Tom Nalen, the Broncos most certainly had the right player.

The seventh-round selection was one of the biggest steals in franchise history, anchoring a line that led a procession of running backs to career years.

Add two Super Bowl rings, five Pro Bowls, and two First-Team All-Pro selections and you have all the criteria required for a date in Canton.

3. Rod Smith

Rod Smith might not have had the swagger of some of his elite receiving contemporaries, but when it comes to consistent, high-class performance, there haven't been many better than #80.

The stats are hugely impressive; 849 regular season catches for 11,389 yards and 68 touchdowns are a fantastic haul. Passing the 1,000-yard barrier eight times,

Smith was voted to the Pro Bowl three times. Add another 49 postseason catches for 860 yards and six touchdowns and you have a hugely impressive career.

What's all the more remarkable about those numbers is that Smith had a slow start to his professional career, grabbing just 22 catches in his first two seasons. Opportunities for an undrafted player are very different from a first-round pick, after all. When the Broncos realized what they had in Smith, he didn't look back.

Both a deep threat and a super-reliable possession receiver, Smith had it all and deserves a Gold Jacket.

2. Randy Gradishar

There's been no more consistently impressive performer for the Broncos on the defensive side of the ball than Randy Gradishar. Which makes it all the more baffling why the selection committee at the Pro Football Hall of Fame hasn't done the decent thing and voted the linebacker in.

In 10 years in Denver, Gradishar was a tackling machine, totaling 2,049 throughout his career including a mammoth 286 in 1978 (a figure that remains a franchise record). A superb run stuffer, Gradishar was also perfectly adept in coverage. Add in 20 interceptions and 13 fumble recoveries and you have a truly great all-round performer. One you can build a defense around.

Gradishar received national recognition after being named the NFL Defensive Player of the Year for 1978. He was also voted to the Pro Bowl seven times and was twice named a First Team All-Pro. The Ohio State alum was granite tough too, not missing a single game in his entire NFL career.

We understand that middle linebacker is considered something of a "plug and play" position in the NFL in the 2020s. It most definitely wasn't in the 1970s and '80s. And in Randy Gradishar, the Broncos benefited from a rock-solid performer, one of the best the game has ever seen.

STOP PRESS: AUGUST 2023 – Gradishar was named a senior finalist for the Pro Football Hall of Fame Class of 2024. About time too.

1. Mike Shanahan

The NFL of today would be a very different beast without the influence of Mike Shanahan. The Shanahan coaching tree contains Zac Taylor, Matt LaFleur, Sean McVay, Mike McDaniel, son Kyle, and many, many more. The wide zone running scheme is a perennial favorite with offensive coordinators and remains hugely successful. That's quite the influence for a coach who hung up his clipboard in 2013.

Of course, Shanahan has plenty of his own achievements to celebrate, chiefly the pair of Super Bowls in 1997 and 1998. There's also the 1994 Super Bowl ring he won with the 49ers as offensive coordinator.

Shanahan also had a huge influence on the Broncos' third Super Bowl title. Head coach Gary Kubiak was a disciple, learning his trade as offensive coordinator under Shanahan.

At the time of writing, Shanahan is one of just three eligible head coaches with multiple Super Bowl wins to have not been inducted in Canton (the others being George Seifert and Tom Coughlin).

Combine the superb success on the field with a hugely influential legacy and Shanahan should be a slam dunk for the Hall of Fame.

Trivia Test

Mike Shanahan spent the final four seasons of his head coaching career with which team?

a) Dallas

b) Philadelphia

c) Washington

Top 5 What Might Have Beens...

There's a 1998 romantic comedy called *Sliding Doors*. The story centers on a London woman and how her life is massively impacted depending on whether or not she gets on a certain subway train. One seemingly tiny decision can have long-lasting implications. The Broncos have had plenty of these *Sliding Doors* moments. Here are the top 5 What Might Have Beens.

5. What if the Broncos hadn't fumbled twice at the goal line in the 2022 season opener at Seattle?

With the Russell Wilson trade fresh in the memory, a road trip to Seattle for the opening game of the 2022 season was always going to be like walking into a buzz-saw. With a home crowd baying for revenge against their former star quarterback, it was possibly the toughest place for Nathaniel Hackett to start his head coaching career.

There were certainly teething problems in Hackett's first game in charge. We saw more flags than at a sailing regatta, and the clock management was questionable to say the least. Despite all that, this was a very winnable game for the Broncos. One that they might have claimed if they hadn't made so many daft mistakes.

The Broncos outgained their opponent 433 yards to 253, Russell Wilson passed for 340 yards with no interceptions, and Denver had the ball seven minutes longer than the Seahawks. How on earth did they lose?

Like many a losing postmortem, turnovers featured heavily. The Broncos fumbled not once but twice at the Seattle goal line in the second half. If they held on to the ball and made it into the end zone just once there, the outcome could have been very different. Brandon McManus' missed 64-yard field goal confirmed a brutal 16-17 loss.

If the Broncos had managed to squeak out a confidence-boosting road win in the season opener, might the season have shaped up better? Perhaps.

4. What if Bennie Fowler hadn't dropped an easy touchdown against the Titans in 2016?

Bennie Fowler is the answer to a great trivia question. Who caught Peyton Manning's final career pass? Fowler snagged the two-point conversion in Super Bowl 50, which put the cherry on top of the 24-10 victory.

The Broncos' Super Bowl defense was on track heading into their Week 14 clash against the Titans. With the defense as sturdy as usual and Trevor Siemian managing the offense, the 8-4 Broncos were right in the hunt for a playoff run.

Trailing 13-7 late in the fourth quarter, Siemian delivered a perfect pass to Fowler in the end zone for a potential game-winning touchdown. Somehow, Fowler managed to drop it and the Broncos were forced to settle for a field goal. Denver had one last chance to win the game, but an A. J. Derby fumble sealed the deal for Tennessee.

Had Fowler held onto the catch, the Broncos would have been 9-4, a game behind in the race for the AFC West and safely in the Wild Card pack.

The Tennessee loss, followed by defeats to New England and Kansas City, derailed that postseason push.

If Fowler hung on, the Broncos would have likely made the playoffs. Then would Gary Kubiak stay as head coach? Fine margins can have huge implications.

3. What if TD hadn't got injured?

Fresh from a 2,000-yard, League MVP year, Terrell Davis was *the* dominant offensive player heading into the 1999 season. The Broncos' Super Bowl defense got off to a disastrous start, though, as they started the season with four straight losses. Compounding that terrible beginning was a season-ending injury to their star rusher.

TD first came to prominence after making an amazing special teams tackle in a preseason game against the 49ers. His career was effectively ended with another tackle, this one following a Brian Griese interception in a Week 4 matchup against the Jets that resulted in two torn knee ligaments. Davis returned from this brutal setback but was a shadow of the player who had terrorized the league pre-injury.

What would have happened if Davis hadn't made that tackle? He started the 1999 season slowly compared to previous years, totaling 211 yards from 67 carries in those first four games. He might not have threatened the giddy heights of 2,000 yards, but you'd still expect Davis to be a hugely successful back.

Mike Shanahan's superb zone blocking scheme created lanes for a host of rushers including Mike Anderson, Reuben Droughns, and Clinton Portis among others. There was every reason to expect an injury-free Davis to do better than all of them.

The running game was never really the issue in the latter years of the Shanahan era, and Davis might not have led the Broncos to more Super Bowl glory. He'd have probably gone on to break a host of records if he had remained healthy, though.

2. What if the Broncos hadn't taken a knee in the Divisional Round playoff against the Ravens?

The Broncos' loss to the Ravens in the 2012 Divisional Round playoff was one of the most brutal in franchise history. Looking back, there's one decision that seems a little strange, especially given the explosiveness of the Peyton Manning-led offense that season.

The Ravens tied the score at 35 apiece courtesy of Jacoby Jones' 70-yard touchdown catch in the final minute of the fourth quarter. Justin Tucker's kickoff resulted in a touchback, giving the Broncos the ball at their own 20-yard line with 31 seconds on the clock and two timeouts in their pocket.

Given the thin Mile High air and Matt Prater's booming leg, getting into field goal range wasn't beyond the realm of possibilities, especially with those two unused timeouts. Instead, the Broncos went the conservative route, took a knee, and sent the game to overtime.

The Broncos offense hadn't quite been at their buccaneering best against the Ravens that night but looking back, the decision to take a knee appears a baffling one.

1. What if the John Elway trade didn't happen?

It's safe to say that the Broncos as an organization and Denver as a city would look very different if the trade to acquire John Elway from Baltimore hadn't happened.

Dan Reeves had shown that he was a competent coach by steering the 1981 Broncos to a 10-6 record with the 38-year-old Craig Morton at quarterback. Steve DeBerg had his moments in a 17-year NFL career but was the epitome of a journeyman quarterback. Both were a million miles from the Elway experience.

We imagine the Broncos being a conservative but always competitive team under Coach Reeves minus the talismanic quarterback. It's hard to imagine them reaching multiple Super Bowls, though.

Without Elway there's no "Drive," no "Helicopter," and likely no back-to-back Super Bowl titles. Without Elway the player, there's probably no Elway the GM either. No Peyton Manning, no No Fly Zone, and no Super Bowl 50.

With the possible exception of Argentine soccer player Diego Maradona in Naples, it's hard to think of a player who has transformed a city quite as much as Elway did Denver.

Trivia Test

Which of the following quarterbacks threw the most touchdown passes while with the Broncos?

a) Teddy Bridgewater

b) Drew Lock

c) Trevor Siemian

Top 5 Pop Culture Cameos

The NFL pops up in all sorts of unusual places these days. Even on this side of the pond, you'll find football players are, if not quite household names, much more recognizable than a generation ago. As one of the biggest and best franchises in the League, the Broncos have made their share of media appearances. Here are the 5 Top Pop Culture Cameos.

5. Doc Brown's Clock in *Back to the Future*

Every good ride needs a quality timepiece, and Doc Brown's DeLorean from time-traveling '80s classic *Back to the Future* had the best on offer – a Broncos alarm clock featuring the classic helmet and D logo.

Was the eccentric scientist an unlikely member of Broncos Country? Screenwriter Bob Gale took up the story in an October 2020 interview with *The Hollywood Reporter*.

"It was just something the set dressers or props people found, it was interesting so we put it in the movie. Is Doc a football fan or a Broncos fan? We know he's a baseball fan, so he could be a football fan. Or maybe he acquired it on a trip to Denver. We know he's not from Denver, but maybe his mother was (his father, remember, was German and originally Von Braun)."[58]

Of course, the Broncos indirectly featured in the sequel, where the villainous Biff takes advantage of and makes a fortune knowing football scores in advance courtesy of the *Grays Sports Almanac*.

4. Last Man Standing

Not to be confused with the Prohibition-era action movie of the same name starring Bruce Willis, *Last Man Standing* is a sitcom that centers on Mike Baxter (played by Tim Allen), an exec at a sporting goods chain based in Colorado.

Working at a sporting goods store and living in Denver, he just had to be a Broncos fan. The show contained plenty of references to football and the Broncos in particular. A classic example was the episode *Gameday Fortunes: Showers*. Which Broncos fan wouldn't be hugely disappointed to discover that a wedding shower was scheduled for the same day as a clash between the Broncos and Chargers?

It might not have quite had the impact of *Home Improvement*, but *Last Man Standing* was a staple of the schedules from 2011 to 2021, picking up five Emmys in the process.

3. Mork, the Male Cheerleader

Who was the Broncos' first male cheerleader? Take a bow, Mork (aka Robin Williams) from the hit TV comedy *Mork and Mindy*, who took the honors during an eccentric 1979 episode.

A spin-off from *Happy Days*, *Mork and Mindy* centered on the adventures of an alien who called Boulder, Colorado home. The most memorable episode for Broncos Country was the one where Williams, sporting the full kit and caboodle, joined the Broncos cheerleaders for an energetic on-field performance.

The scenes were filmed during a 45-10 win over the Patriots in November 1979. Looking at the skimpy outfits they were wearing that day, they must have been pretty chilly.

This must go down as one of the strangest performances ever witnessed at Mile High Stadium.

2. When TD Went to *Sesame Street*

An all-time great meets an all-time great. The greats in question here were Terrell Davis and Big Bird from *Sesame Street*. TD was invited to appear on the classic children's TV show during the 1998 season. Nothing controversial about that, surely? Well, not quite.

The appearance was scheduled for the Monday after the Broncos played the Giants in New York. Unfortunately, the team's 13-game unbeaten run was ended by Big Blue, and head coach Mike Shanahan was not a happy bunny. Instead of allowing him to stay in New York for the *Sesame Street* appearance, TD was ordered to fly back to Denver with the rest of the team for a Monday workout.

Davis ended up flying back to New York after that Monday workout, filming for *Sesame Street* on Tuesday and then returning to Denver for the scheduled Wednesday practice. It all worked out swimmingly in the end as the Broncos went on to claim a second Super Bowl title and TD got to complete a lifelong dream.

Interviewed by DenverBroncos.com in 2017, TD jokingly rated Sesame Street as the pinnacle of his career. "Yeah, 'Sesame Street' might be up there. That might be number one. 'Sesame Street,' then the Hall of Fame, then the other stuff."[59]

1. The New Owner of the Broncos is...Homer Simpson

The Broncos gained an unlikely new owner in 1996. In an episode of *The Simpsons* titled "You Only Move Twice," Homer Simpson was gifted the Broncos ownership by a James Bond-style supervillain named Hank Scorpio.

The family patriarch was typically disappointed with his gift, hoping instead to have received the then far more successful Dallas Cowboys.

The Broncos would have the last laugh here. Since Homer assumed his fictional ownership of the team, the Broncos have won three Super Bowls and the Cowboys none. In head-to-head matchups since the episode aired in November 1996, the Broncos are a perfect 7-0 against America's Team.

Let's hope the Penners are as successful as the Simpsons in the ownership stakes.

Trivia Test

Which Hollywood star played Broncos legend Floyd Little in the 2008 movie *The Express*?

a) Chadwick Boseman

b) Don Cheadle

c) Jamie Foxx

Top 5 Broncos Books

Social media and websites are great for when you want to keep up with the latest Broncos-related news and opinion. Sometimes, you really want to take a truly deep dive into a subject, and only a book will do. Here are Five Broncos Books well worth perusing.

5. *If These Walls Could Talk: Denver Broncos: Stories from the Denver Broncos Sideline, Locker Room, and Press Box* by Dave Logan with Arnie Stapleton

After a lengthy playing career and an even longer spell as a broadcaster, few people are better placed to take readers behind the scenes with the Broncos than Dave Logan.

The wide receiver turned play-by-play man teamed up with Denver-based Associated Press football writer Arnie Stapleton to compile a collection of some of his best Broncos-related stories in *If These Walls Could Talk: Denver Broncos*.

You'll find cameos from many of the biggest names in franchise history and plenty of superb tales. Expect outlandish characters, tall stories, and plenty of giggles. It's all told in Logan's homely style and is a highly entertaining read.

4. *77: Denver, The Broncos, and a Coming of Age* by Terry Frei

The Broncos' run to the Super Bowl in 1977 didn't just transform the team, it also helped transform the city of Denver. Terry Frei tells the tale of that truly amazing season in *77: Denver, The Broncos, and a Coming of Age*.

This isn't just a book about football, although there's plenty on that record-breaking season. It also tells a wider story of how the Broncos helped turned Denver from something of a provincial backwater to a powerhouse of the American West.

Expect the inside story on the rise of Red Miller's team from the M and M Connection through to Lyle Alzado, Tom Jackson, and the Orange Crush. You'll also get something of a history lesson here too.

The best sports books are about much more than the sport, and Frei's *77* is a fine example of that.

3. *A Few Seconds of Panic: A Sportswriter Plays in the NFL* by Stefan Fatsis

George Plimpton literally wrote the book on what it was like to be an enthusiastic amateur thrust into the spotlight with the big boys of professional sport. Plimpton boxed with Archie Moore, pitched at Yankee Stadium, and played center for the Detroit Lions.

The Broncos got the Plimpton-style treatment from sportswriter Stefan Fatsis in *A Few Seconds of Panic*. The author had previously gone deep into the world of competitive Scrabble in the highly entertaining *Word Freak*.

Given his fortysomething age and less than statuesque physique, the natural position to try was kicker. Offering readers an up-close and personal look at how the NFL sausage is made, Fatsis spent three months training with the Broncos.

The result is an often amusing peek behind the pro football curtain. Having followed Fatsis' travails, you'll have a newfound respect every time Brandon McManus boots one through the uprights.

2. *Elway: A Relentless Life* by Jason Cole

No man has had a greater impact on the Denver Broncos than John Elway, but what makes the great man tick? Jason Cole tries to see beyond the legend in *Elway: A Relentless Life*.

Tracing Elway's journey from high school phenom to hot college prospect to NFL superstar and beyond, it's an in-depth and enlightening read.

Superbly researched and packed full of detail, Cole reveals plenty about Elway's career in Denver from his often-fiery relationships with coaches Dan Reeves and Mike Shanahan through to his decision-making processes as general manager.

A Relentless Life offers a portrait of Elway the man rather than just Elway the quarterback. How he rebounded from the breakdown of his marriage and the deaths of his father and twin sister and returned to football to steer the Broncos to another Super Bowl title as an exec.

We waited a long time for the definitive Elway biography, and in *A Relentless Life*, Cole has delivered it.

1. *Slow Getting Up: A Story of NFL Survival from the Bottom of the Pile* by Nate Jackson

There's plenty written about the superstars of the game. What about those players lower down the food chain trying to make it as a pro? That ground's eye perspective is what's offered in Nate Jackson's superb *Slow Getting Up*.

If you're not familiar with the name, that's no surprise. Jackson caught just 27 passes throughout the entirety of his six-year NFL career, the majority of which he spent with the Broncos.

That journeyman status makes for a terrific book, though, offering readers a warts and all look at what life is like for players battling for a roster spot. The injuries, the meetings, the travel, the groupies, the teammates, the coaches, the constant stress.

If all that sounds like a grind, it is. But there's no greater buzz than taking to the field at a packed stadium with a roaring crowd.

Jackson's career as a wide receiver and tight end didn't really hit the heights, but in *Slow Getting Up*, he delivered one of the best football books you'll read.

Trivia Test

Whose 2012 autobiography was called *Promises to Keep*?

a) Tom Jackson

b) Floyd Little

c) Karl Mecklenburg

1. Rich Karlis - https://vault.si.com/vault/2000/07/24/rich-karlis-barefoot-kicker-january-19-1987

2. Brandon McManus - https://www.denverpost.com/2014/11/24/hochman-broncos-must-cut-unreliable-place-kicker-brandon-mcmanus/

3. Bill Romanowski - https://www.tmz.com/2014/01/28/bill-romanowski-dirty-player-sometimes-dave-meggett/

4. Dennis Smith - https://buffalonews.com/sports/bills/trade-secrets-thurman-thomas-shares-all-with-a-bills-rookie/article_888556f2-2401-5605-b067-c664ed785c58.html

5. Steve Atwater - https://apnews.com/article/sports-nfl-super-bowl-denver-broncos-eaa7a8a026d8f0762c327579f2bbe972T

6. Spencer Larsen - https://www.espn.co.uk/nfl/news/story?id=3706395

7. Kendall Hinton - https://twitter.com/kendall_hinton2/status/1413234495508164608

8. Pat Surtain - https://twitter.com/nextgenstats/status/1465106932595789826?lang=en

9. Brian Griese - https://www.espn.com/nfl/news/2000/1114/876898.html#:~:text=The%20Raiders%20had%20an%2011,finish%20the%20final%20three%20quarters

10. Derek Wolfe - https://twitter.com/mikeklis/status/1612603454282948609

11. Lyle Alzado - https://news.google.com/newspapers?nid=1346&dat=19790716&id=Oo0sAAAAIBAJ&sjid=9_oDAAAAIBAJ&pg=6864,196050&hl=en

12. Vernon Davis - https://eu.usatoday.com/story/sports/nfl/2016/01/25/together-a-decade-kubiak-and-daniels-heading-to-super-bowl/79322282/

13. Rulon Jones - https://milehighsports.com/karl-mecklenburg-thinks-rulon-jones-deserves-the-broncos-ring-of-fame-call/

14. The Helicopter - https://vault.si.com/vault/1998/02/02/seven-up-showing-more-grit-than-prowess-john-elway-executed-a-brilliant-game-plan-in-the-broncos-stunning-super-bowl-win-over-the-packers

15. The Immaculate Deflection - https://www.denverbroncos.com/news/immaculate-deflection-remembered-8721621

16. 1996 Loss to the Jaguars - https://www.denverpost.com/2013/01/11/jaguars-handed-broncos-a-painful-playoff-loss-16-years-ago-in-denver/

17. Double Overtime Disaster Against the Ravens - https://www.nfl.com/news/joe-flacco-proves-his-worth-to-baltimore-ravens-in-win-0ap1000000125378

18. Snowball Game - https://www.49ers.com/news/75-for-75-the-snowball-game-ray-wersching-kicker-denver-broncos#:~:text=Referee%20Jim%20Tunney%20later%20explained,nearly%20insignificant%20pre%2Dhalftime%20moment

19. Buffalo Stance - https://www.deseret.com/1997/10/27/19342098/broncos-survive-snow-bills-23-20#:~:text=Safety%20Steve%20Atwater%20needed%20a,%2C%22%20coach%20Mike%20Shanahan%20said

20. Wesley Woodyard - https://twitter.com/WoodDro52/status/1360395548839313408?ref_src=twsrc%5Etfw%7Ctwcamp%5Etweetembed%7Ctwterm%5E1360395548839313408%7Ctwgr%5Eff4c33f19e5552dfcd8732323272fb2ec6db9bd4%7Ctwcon%5Es1_&ref_url=https%3A%2F%2Ftitanswire.usatoday.com%2F2021%2F02%2F12%2Ftennessee-titans-wesley-woodyard-rescue-car-accident%2F

21. Steve Watson - https://books.google.co.uk/books?id=4P41DwAAQBAJ&pg=PA239&lpg=PA239&dq=babe+parilli+&source=bl&ots=cgRZgGgPME&sig=ACfU3U0n3oEH0BYlmfi4dnShcr5fVIpTfA&hl=en&sa=X&redir_esc=y#v=onepage&q=babe%20parilli%20&f=false

22. Chris Harris Jr. - https://www.theplayerstribune.com/articles/chris-harris-broncos-undrafted

23. Gary Zimmerman - https://www.denverbroncos.com/news/way-back-when-the-greatness-of-gary-zimmerman

24. Tyrone Braxton - https://www.denverbroncos.com/news/where-are-they-now-tyrone-braxton-19399614

25. Tom Nalen - https://twitter.com/johnelway/status/337308030892912640

26. Karl Mecklenburg - https://www.denverbroncos.com/news/tales-from-the-draft-the-call-that-woke-up-karl-mecklenburg-in-the-12th-round

27. Shannon Sharpe - https://www.denverbroncos.com/news/tales-from-the-draft-why-the-broncos-overlooked-a-bad-combine-workout-and-tweene

28. Peyton Manning - https://play.hbomax.com/episode/urn:hbo:episode:GYR_Tgg7EkI98ggEAAAAG

29. Terrell Davis - https://www.foxsports.com/stories/nfl/my-big-game-moment-terrell-davis-dealt-with-his-pain

30. Tim Tebow - https://eu.usatoday.com/story/sports/2018/06/08/tim-tebow-kneeling-national-anthem/686533002/

31. Von Miller - https://apnews.com/article/062c704b2ad44c07be31f54848f84791

32. Mile High Salute - https://www.denverpost.com/2017/08/05/terrell-davis-mile-high-salute/

33. Jim Turner - https://history.denverbroncos.com/1977/10/the-broncos-greatest-gadget-play/

34. Aqib Talib - https://milehighsports.com/aqib-talib-explains-what-spurned-his-beef-with-michael-crabtree-and-how-it-was-resolved/

35. Shannon Sharpe - https://news.google.com/newspapers?nid=1298&dat=19981206&id=G_EyAAAAIBAJ&sjid=yAgGAAAAIBAJ&pg=5223,1219685&hl=en

36. Shannon Sharpe - https://books.google.co.uk/books?id=AmHZDwAAQBAJ&pg=PT288&lpg=PT288&dq=shannon+sharpe+derrick+thomas+phone+number&source=bl&ots=Ukrje9LLOY&sig=ACfU3U24rxXpnIOlutPX0cwJaqb3qps3vw&hl=en&sa=X&ved=2ahUKEwj3xLDeouf7AhWSfMAKHZmTDEYQ6AF6BAg5EAM#v=onepage&q=shannon%20sharpe%20derrick%20thomas%20phone%20number&f=false

37. Rich Jackson - https://www.youtube.com/watch?v=lNdcOGNpTGU

38. Steve Atwater - https://www.denverpost.com/2019/01/20/steve-atwater-hall-of-famer-says-charlie-waters/#:~:text=The%20%E2%80%9CSmiling%20Assassin%E2%80%9D%20nickname%20was,up%20smiling%2C%E2%80%9D%20Waters%20recalled

39. Steve Atwater - https://www.denverpost.com/2019/01/20/steve-atwater-hall-of-famer-says-charlie-waters/#:~:text=The%20%E2%80%9CSmiling%20Assassin%E2%80%9D%20nickname%20was,up%20smiling%2C%E2%80%9D%20Waters%20recalled

40. Elvis Dumervil - https://www.piersongrant.com/prestige-estates-owner-oversees-renovation-of-prestige-waterfront/

41. Rich Karlis - https://www.barefootbroncowoodworking.com/about-rich-karlis

42. Jake Plummer - https://www.cbsnews.com/colorado/news/from-nfl-quarterback-to-mushroom-farmer-jake-plummers-journey-from-the-gridiron-to-the-fields-of-fort-lupton/

43. Broncos Ditch the Orange Uniforms - https://theathletic.com/249283/2018/02/22/behold-the-batwing-how-the-denver-broncos-and-nike-teamed-up-and-forever-changed-uniform-design/

44. Broncos Ditch the Orange Uniforms - https://www.tampabay.com/archive/1997/10/07/city-wore-a-frown-over-new-uniforms/

45. Bill Romanowski Spits at J. J. Stokes - https://www.deseret.com/1997/12/18/19352078/romanowski-apologizes-calls-spitting-inexcusable

46. Dan Reeves and John Elway - https://vault.si.com/vault/1993/08/02/happy-days-as-the-era-of-wade-phillips-dawns-in-denver-the-broncos-are-all-smiles

47. Dan Reeves and John Elway - https://www.chron.com/sports/texans/article/Elway-ready-to-make-up-with-Reeves-1966079.php

48. Dan Reeves and John Elway - https://twitter.com/johnelway/status/1477341409921290242

49. John Elway and Terry Bradshaw - https://twitter.com/masedenver/status/1539438564232118274

50. John Elway and Terry Bradshaw - https://www.washingtonpost.com/archive/sports/1990/01/25/move-over-montana-its-elway-bradshaw/cce321c9-165a-47c3-a1ed-cc232c9808f1/

51. Josh McDaniels and Everyone - https://profootballtalk.nbcsports.com/2022/02/01/josh-mcdaniels-i-failed-in-denver-because-i-didnt-know-how-to-work-with-people/

52. Chauncey Billups - https://www.denverbroncos.com/video/billups-born-with-orange-blood-13303781

53. Chauncey Billups - https://www.denverpost.com/2014/01/23/hochman-chauncey-billups-fondly-embraces-we-the-broncos-nation/

54. Orange Hush - https://www.latimes.com/archives/la-xpm-1998-jan-17-sp-9293-story.html

55. Orange Hush - https://www.chicagotribune.com/news/ct-xpm-1998-01-21-9801210017-story.html

56. The Three Amigos - https://www.denverpost.com/2013/09/04/broncos-original-three-amigos-ride-again-living-on-in-nfl-history/

57. Louis Wright - https://www.si.com/nfl/talkoffame/nfl/state-your-case-louis-wright

58. Doc Brown's Clock in Back to the Future - https://www.hollywoodreporter.com/movies/movie-news/back-to-the-future-screenwriter-bob-gale-explains-docs-denver-broncos-clock-4080397/

59. Terrell Davis on Sesame Street - https://www.denverbroncos.com/news/the-pick-six-hall-of-famer-terrell-davis-says-sesame-street-appearance--19101706

Trivia Test Answers

Quarterbacks – Jake Plummer with 499 yards against Atlanta in 2004.

Running Backs – Floyd Little has the most Pro Bowl selections with five.

Wide Receivers – Demaryius Thomas has the most catches in postseason games.

Pass Rushers – Von Miller's middle name is B'Vsean.

Ball Hawks – Champ Bailey and Steve Atwater are the two Denver DBs with eight Pro Bowls.

Returners – Vaughn Hebron has the record for the most kickoff returns in franchise history.

Kickers – Connor Barth was the unlucky kicker who lost his job despite an impressive record.

Hardest Hitters – Dennis Smith has the most sacks by a Broncos defensive back with 15.

Rookie Seasons – Mike Anderson's 80-yard rush against Seattle is the longest by a Broncos rookie.

Versatile Players – John Lynch was named the GM of the San Francisco 49ers.

Backup Quarterbacks – Trevor Siemian's 11 wins are the most by a Broncos quarterback in the post-Manning era.

Speedsters – Champ Bailey's given first name was Roland.

Fleeting Favorites – Tim Tebow was the winner of the Heisman Trophy.

Tough Guys – Darren Drozdov was the footballer turned wrestler.

One and Done Seasons – Lady Gaga was the National Anthem singer at Super Bowl 50.

Unsung Players – Sammy Winder is tied for second (with John Elway) for the most rushing yards in playoff games with 461.

Did They Play in Denver – Sammy Winder caught Tony Dorsett's only career touchdown pass.

Super Bowl Moments – T. J. Ward picked of a Cam Newton pass in Super Bowl 50.

Craziest Finishes – Best known for his time in Indy, Brandon Stokley started (and ended) his NFL career in Baltimore.

Playoff Moments (Offense) – Clarence Kay is the other tight end alongside Owen Daniels to score two TDs in a single playoff game.

Playoff Moments (Defense) – Von Miller with 6.5 has the most sacks by a Bronco in postseason games.

Crushing Losses – The Broncos blew a 24-point lead in a 31-34 loss to New England.

Weather Games – The Broncos have a losing record on artificial turf and are a horrible 1-10 in postseason games played on artificial turf.

Wins Over the Patriots – Knowshon Moreno with 224 yards in 2013 is the only Bronco to rush for 200 yards in a single game against New England.

Undrafted Free Agents – Running back Philip Lindsay was the first undrafted rookie to receive Pro Bowl honors.

Terrific Trades – John Elway was selected by the New York Yankees in the 1981 MLB Draft.

Free Agent Signings (Offense) – With 34 TDs, Demaryius Thomas was Peyton Manning's top touchdown target while with the Broncos.

Free Agent Signings (Defense) – Alfred Williams had the most sacks of the trio with 28.5.

Terrible Trades – Jerry Jeudy caught Russell Wilson's first touchdown pass as a Bronco.

Head Coaches – Red Miller's given first name was Robert.

Head Coaching Calamities – Josh McDaniels at .393 has a better win percentage than Vic Fangio's .388 or Vance Joseph's .344.

Draft Steals – TD made his amazing special teams tackle in a game played in Tokyo.

Draft Busts – Paxton Lynch played in college for the Memphis Tigers.

Free Agent Flops – Melvin Gordon played for the Chargers before joining the Broncos.

Comebacks – The Broncos took Drew Lock in the second round of the 2019 NFL Draft.

Celebrations – DeMarcus Ware appeared on *Dancing with the Stars* in 2018, finishing in a respectable seventh position.

Trick Plays – Arthur Marshall was the receiver with two touchdown passes in 1992 and 1993.

Colorado Connections – Ben Garland has served with Air Force.

Big Man Touchdowns – Defensive end Harald Hasselbach was born in Amsterdam in The Netherlands.

Talkers – Shannon Sharpe enjoyed a frank exchange of views with members of the Memphis Grizzlies.

Individual Player Nicknames – Chicken was the nickname of Tyrone Braxton.

Post Football Careers – The last player other than Von Miller to register double-digit sacks in successive seasons was Trevor Pryce in 1999 and 2000.

Most Shocking Moments – In 1960 and 1961, the Broncos wore yellow and brown home uniforms.

Feuds and Fallouts – Peyton Manning was the last quarterback to lead the Broncos to a win over Kansas City.

Famous Fans – The famous horse statue that sits atop Mile High Stadium is called Bucky.

Group Nicknames – Ricky Nattiel was the first-round draft pick. Johnson and Jackson were selected in the second and sixth rounds, respectively.

They Should Be in the Hall of Fame – Mike Shanahan spent the final four seasons as a head coach in Washington.

What Might Have Beens – Trevor Siemian threw 30 TDs followed by 25 for Lock and 18 for Bridgewater.

Pop Culture Cameos – The late Chadwick Boseman played Floyd "The Franchise" Little in the 2008 movie *The Express*, which was based on the life of Heisman Trophy winner Ernie Davis.

Books – Floyd Little's 2012 autobiography was called *Promises to Keep*.

Bibiography

Books

Cole, Jason – *Elway: A Relentless Life* (Hachette Books, 2020)

Denver Broncos 2022 Media Guide

Fleder, Rob (Editor) – *Sports Illustrated: Great Football Writing* (Sports Illustrated Books, 2006)

Frei, Terry – *77: Denver, The Broncos, and a Coming of Age* (Taylor Trade Publishing, 2009)

Howell, Brian – *100 Things Broncos Fans Should Know & Do Before They Die* (Triumph Books, 2016)

Jackson, Nate – *Slow Getting Up: A Story of NFL Survival from the Bottom of the Pile* (Harper, 2013)

Klis, Mike – *The 50 Greatest Players in Denver Broncos History* (Lyons Press, 2017)

Logan, Dave and Stapleton, Arnie – *If These Walls Could Talk: Denver Broncos: Stories from the Denver Broncos Sideline, Locker Room, and Press Box* (Triumph Books, 2020)

Mason, Andrew – *Tales from the Denver Broncos Sideline: A Collection of the Greatest Broncos Stories Ever Told* (Sports Publishing, 2017)

Myers, Gary – *Coaching Confidential: Inside the Fraternity of NFL Coaches* (Crown Archetype, 2012)

Saccomano, Jim – *Denver Broncos: The Complete Illustrated History* (MVP Books, 2009)

Walker, Ray – *The Ultimate Denver Broncos Trivia Book* (HRP House, 2020)

Websites

BleacherReport.com

BroncosWire.USAToday.com

CBSSports.com

DenverBroncos.com

DenverPost.com

ESPN.com

KDVR.com

MileHighReport.com

NFL.com

PFF.com

PredominantlyOrange.com

Pro-Football-Reference.com

SBNation.com

SI.com

TheAthletic.com

YardBreaker.com

YouTube.com

Acknowledgements

Many thanks to editor David Aretha for his perceptive comments and suggestions. Likewise, Colum Cronin from the excellent Dublin to Denver podcast. Thanks also to David Luxton, Heidi Grant, Stuart Kennedy, Bill Rankin, Ken and Veronica Bradshaw, Steph, James, Ben and Will Roe. Finally, a big thank you to designer Graham Nash aka Headfuzz by Grimboid.

About the Author

Chris Bradshaw has written more than 30 quiz book including titles on the NFL, college football, golf, tennis, Formula One, Moto GP and cycling. He has also written on cricket for The Times (of London) as well as on soccer, darts and poker.

ALSO BY CHRIS BRADSHAW

Formula One Trivia Quiz Book

MotoGP Trivia Quiz Book

Golf Trivia Quiz Book

Tennis Trivia Quiz Book

Boston Red Sox Trivia Quiz Book

Chicago Cubs Trivia Quiz Book

New York Yankees Trivia Quiz Book

Baltimore Ravens Trivia Quiz Book

Chicago Bears Trivia Quiz Book

Cincinnati Bengals Trivia Quiz Book

Dallas Cowboys Trivia Quiz Book

Denver Broncos Trivia Quiz Book

Green Bay Packers Trivia Quiz Book

Kansas City Chiefs Trivia Quiz Book

Miami Dolphins Trivia Quiz Book

Minnesota Vikings Trivia Quiz Book

New England Patriots Trivia Quiz Book

New York Giants Trivia Quiz Book

Ohio State Buckeyes Trivia Quiz Book

Philadelphia Eagles Trivia Quiz Book

Pittsburgh Steelers Trivia Quiz Book

San Francisco 49ers Trivia Quiz Book

Seattle Seahawks Trivia Quiz Book

Tampa Bay Buccaneers Trivia Quiz Book

Washington Commanders Trivia Quiz Book

Georgia Bulldogs Trivia Quiz Book

Michigan Wolverines Trivia Quiz Book

The Times Cricket Quiz Book

The Sun Darts Quiz Book

Made in the USA
Las Vegas, NV
12 September 2023

77462736R00152